ESPECIALLY FOR

....

FROM

....

DATE

....

3-MINUTE
DEVOTIONS

for GIRLS

SHILOH ! kidz

An Imprint of Barbour Publishing, Inc.

INTRODUCTION

What a busy girl you are! You have so much going on—school, friends, sports, and family activities. There's not always time to sit and read, read, read. That's what makes this devotional so perfect for you! These little three-minute readings will give you all of the inspiration you need before heading out to school or to play. *And* you'll be learning a lot about yourself and God in a short time! Here's what each power-packed devotion looks like:

Minute 1: Reflect on God's Word.
Minute 2: Read real-life application and encouragement.
Minute 3: Pray.

Of course, these devotions aren't supposed to take the place of regular Bible reading. They're just a fun jump start to help you form a habit of spending time with God every day.

Here's a really cool idea: Why not share what you learn in this devotional with your school friends, family members, and even the girls you don't usually talk to? Everyone needs inspiration and encouragement, you know. So, girl, what are you waiting for? Let's dive in and discover how three minutes a day could change your entire life!

Your word is a lamp to guide my feet
and a light for my path.
PSALM 119:105 NLT

THE PICTURE OF PERFECTION

For everyone has sinned; we all fall short of God's glorious standard. Yet God, with undeserved kindness, declares that we are righteous. He did this through Christ Jesus when he freed us from the penalty for our sins.

ROMANS 3:23–24 NLT

Have you ever met someone who seems to be perfect in every way? Perfect grades. Perfect clothes. Perfect family. Doesn't seem fair, does it? How come she and her life are perfect and you and your life aren't?

Truth is, no one and no thing is perfect—except God. Some people and their lives might seem that way, but they're really not. And it's because people are not perfect that we need God so much! So don't let your flaws and your mess-ups keep you from realizing that you are all God wants you to be. After all, He doesn't expect you to be perfect. (What a relief, right?)

So does that mean you shouldn't keep aiming for excellence? Of course not! God wants you to do the best you can. But remember that even when you mess up (and you will), you can run back to Him and ask for forgiveness and guidance. He'll forgive all of your sins then whisper, "I love you, precious girl! Now walk this way."

Dear Lord, thank You for not expecting me to be perfect! It helps to know You will always love me, in spite of my mess-ups!

PARTING THE RED SEA

*The waters were divided, and the Israelites went through the sea on
dry ground, with a wall of water on their right and on their left.*
EXODUS 14:21-22 NIV

Have you ever read the Old Testament story about the Israelites (God's
people) and the Red Sea? They were being chased by the Egyptians, their
enemy, when Moses led the Israelites to the edge of the sea. They knew they
couldn't go back. The pharaoh and his chariots were right behind them. So
they really needed to get across to the land on the other side. Do you think
they took a boat? Maybe they swam? Went across a bridge? Nope. God
parted the Red Sea! The waters actually separated, and dry land appeared.
The Israelites walked across with water standing on both sides! When the
Egyptians came along behind them, the waters went back to normal again.
God protected His people!

Did you know that God still parts waters for us today? Not the Red Sea, of
course, but He makes impossible things happen every day. He heals people's
diseases. Answers prayers. Performs miracles. All sorts of things! We can
talk to Him anytime we want to, and He listens. He also speaks to us (in our
hearts), so we need to be listening for His voice. Who knows! He might just
be getting ready to part the waters for you too!

Dear Lord, I love reading about the miracles in the Bible, but it gets
me even more excited to know You still perform miracles today.
Thank You for answering my prayers, Father!

YOU ARE A MASTERPIECE

*Still, GOD, you are our Father. We're the clay and
you're our potter: All of us are what you made us.*
ISAIAH 64:8 MSG

If you've ever read the book of Genesis, you know that God created the heavens and the earth then all of the creatures on the earth, including a man named Adam. From man He took a rib and (while Adam slept) created a woman named Eve. It's amazing to think of how God decided we would look: two legs, two arms, two eyes, one mouth. Wowza!

The cool thing is, we're created in His image. Does this mean God has two legs, two arms, two eyes, and one mouth? Nope. But even if we don't know for sure what He looks like, it does mean that we are like Him in other ways—we have His heart for people, His love for our families, His joy, even in the hard times. We also have His good attitude, no matter how difficult things get.

If you're having trouble "being" like your Daddy, God, then ask for His help. Say, "Show me how to be like You, Lord!" and He will. Before long, you'll look so much like Him that people will know you're His child. They will want to know how they can be like Him too!

Oh, how fun to be like our Daddy, God!

Lord, I want to be like You! I won't know what You
look like until I see You face-to-face in heaven, but for now,
give me Your heart, Your love, and Your attitude!

A LITTLE CONFIDENCE GOES A LONG, LONG WAY

Be on your guard; stand firm in the faith; be courageous; be strong.
1 CORINTHIANS 16:13 NIV

God wants you to be courageous, from the inside out. In other words, He doesn't want you to brag about having confidence. He wants you to actually be confident!

Maybe you're one of those girls who isn't very confident. Your knees shake whenever you're asked to do something difficult, such as standing up in front of the class or speaking in public. That's okay! God can use you, and your confidence will grow over time. Start praying now, and ask God to show you how to believe—not in yourself but in Him. Then know and understand that the Lord will give you the courage to boldly do what He asks of you. And keep in mind that if you start applying some of that God-given confidence and boldness now, you will be more able to face others with courage when you're grown up. You won't have to wonder what others are saying about you or whether they think you fit in with the group. None of that will matter. A confident girl is blessed because she knows who she is in Christ and doesn't spend much time worrying about what others think about her.

I don't want to shiver and shake, Lord!

I want to be firm, courageous, and strong!
Give me Your confidence so I can do great things for You!

10

ALL GROWN UP

But the LORD said to me, "Do not say, 'I am too young.' You must go
to everyone I send you to and say whatever I command you."
JEREMIAH 1:7 NIV

When you were a little girl, did you ever play "grown-up"? It was a lot of fun, right? Wearing your mom's high heels. . .dancing around the house in frilly tutus. It's a blast to act like a big girl.

Sometimes we get so excited about what it's going to be like when we're older that we forget God created children for a reason. Being young is fun! God is glad that you're not grown up yet, and He's in no hurry to get you there!

Don't ever look down on yourself because you're young. This breaks God's heart. Don't ever say, "But I'm just a kid! What can I do for God?" The truth is, you can do a lot more than you know, and He wants you—no, He needs you—to understand that you don't have to wait till you're grown up to tell others about Him. So start now. Right where you are. Kick off those high heels. Grab your tennis shoes. . .and get running!

Lord, sometimes I want to be a grown-up. It seems like being an adult
will be more fun. Remind me how much You long for me to go on
being a kid. This is an awesome time in my life!

WANDERING IN THE DESERT

The LORD said to Moses, "How long will these people treat me with contempt? How long will they refuse to believe in me, in spite of all the signs I have performed among them?"

NUMBERS 14:11 NIV

. . . .

Have you ever read the Bible story about the Israelites (God's people) leaving the country of Egypt, headed for the Promised Land? They spent years and years and years in the desert, wandering around. . .lost! Crazy, because it wasn't really that far to Israel (the Promised Land). They could've gotten there much sooner if they had just listened to God's directions!

Have you ever wandered in the desert? Oh, not a real desert, of course. But have you ever listened to God's instruction then stepped out in faith, only to feel lost and afraid? Sometimes we're really bold at first then get scared and lost later.

When God gives us directions, we can trust Him all the way through the journey. Don't stop moving when you feel lost and afraid. Just call out to Him and ask Him to guide you to the next place you need to go. He will do it!

. . . .

Lord, I don't want to wander in the desert like the Israelites.
I want to hear Your voice and move in the direction
You tell me to go. Thank You for leading me.

CASTLE ON A CLOUD

In the beginning God created the heavens and the earth. Now the
earth was formless and empty, darkness was over the surface of
the deep, and the Spirit of God was hovering over the waters.
GENESIS 1:1–2 NIV

Have you ever been accused of being a dreamer? Someone who has her head in the clouds? Your imagination works overtime and you make up story after story? There's nothing wrong with having a great imagination or dreaming up imaginary friends and tall tales. God is pretty creative too! He created the whole world, after all!

Think about that for a moment. God, the Creator of absolutely everything, spoke a few words and the whole world came into existence! He must have quite an imagination! Look at giraffes, for instance. And penguins. And think about the colors of the rainbow! Yes, we serve a creative God. And because we're created in His image, we are creative too!

It's okay to dream, sweet girl. Using your imagination is fun! Just make sure you keep your feet on the ground and your heart close to God's. He will take you to all sorts of lovely places in this life—and beyond.

Father, thank You for giving me an imagination! I'm so glad that I'm creative like You. Help me use my imagination to accomplish great things for You!

TWiNKLE, TWiNKLE, LiTTLE STAR

*"You are the light of the world. A town built
on a hill cannot be hidden."*

MATTHEW 5:14 NIV

Remember that song you used to sing when you were really little: "Twinkle, Twinkle, Little Star"? Although it is a sweet little song about stars in the sky, it can serve as a reminder to Christians that God wants us to twinkle—to shine for Him—so that others will see our light and be drawn to Him. Think about it like this: if you're shining down on the darkness (sin), then others will see that you're different. Being different is a good thing when you're reflecting God's light. No point in hiding your faith from others. Oh, no! Let them know that you love Jesus—in good times and bad. Shine His light so that others can come to know and glow in Him too!

Remember, God is the author of light! That means He made light in the first place. The Creator of the sun, moon, and stars is your guide! And He calls you to be a reflection of His light, whether you're walking through a sunny season or a dark one. So. . .twinkle, twinkle!

Father, sometimes I'm afraid to shine my light. I worry that my
friends will make fun of me. Please give me the courage to go on
shining, even when it's hard. I want to twinkle for You!

FALSELY ACCUSED

"No tool that is made to fight against you will do well.
And you will prove wrong every tongue that says you are guilty.
This is the gift given to the servants of the Lord. I take
away their guilt and make them right," says the Lord.

ISAIAH 54:17 NLV

Has anyone ever accused you of doing something that you didn't really do? Maybe your sister's favorite doll disappeared and she said, "Hey, why did you take my doll?" Or maybe your teacher thought she saw you looking at another student's test paper—but you hadn't.

Being falsely accused stinks. You try to let the accusing person know that you are innocent, but she doesn't always believe you. So you try again, but she still isn't buying it.

Here's some good news: when you're truly innocent, God knows it. Even if no one else believes you, He does. He knows your heart and He sees that you have done nothing wrong. If you are being accused falsely, ask God to bring the truth to light so that others can see it. You can depend on this scripture: "No tool [weapon] that is made to fight against you will do well." And sooner or later, every false accusation against you will be proven wrong. So hang in there, girl. Your day is coming. The truth will come out.

Lord, I don't like to be falsely accused. It hurts my feelings.
Yet I feel like there's nothing I can do. Thank You for reminding
me that the truth will come out sooner or later.

WALKING ON WATER

Shortly before dawn Jesus went out to them,
walking on the lake. When the disciples saw him
walking on the lake, they were terrified.
MATTHEW 14:25–26 NIV

Have you ever walked through a tough situation—one that was really, really tough? Perhaps you've experienced the death of a loved one or have suffered through a major illness. During these types of really hard seasons, we need supernatural faith. Some people would call it walking-on-water faith.

Have you read the New Testament story of Peter? He was one of Jesus' disciples (followers). One night he and the other disciples were in a boat and a howling windstorm blew up. Terrifying! The waves grew very rough!

The men were afraid. Peter saw Jesus out on the water. . .walking! (Can you imagine if you saw one of your friends walking on top of the water?) Jesus asked Peter to join Him. Then a miracle happened. Peter took a few steps and he too found himself walking upon the water! But then, when Peter took his eyes off Jesus, he became afraid and started sinking! He yelled out to Jesus, and immediately Jesus caught him.

We can learn a lot from this story. If we keep our eyes on God during the really tough times, He will give us the faith to do impossible things. Wow!

Lord, sometimes I need walking-on-water faith. I need to believe that You can help me do impossible things. Give me that kind of faith, I pray!

THE EAGER BEAVER

May the favor of the Lord our God rest on us;
establish the work of our hands for us—yes,
establish the work of our hands.

PSALM 90:17 NIV

Are you an eager beaver? One who's chomping at the bit to get the task done? Wonderful! When your attitude is right, you're capable of accomplishing much more. Allow your God-given eagerness to drive you to do great things for Him!

God loves hard workers. He loves watching you try new things and accomplish goals. Whether you're great at sports or art, writing or dance, doesn't matter! He enjoys watching you learn, learn, learn. He also loves it when you work at home, helping your mom and dad around the house or keeping your room clean. All of these things are pleasing to God. How wonderful to please your Daddy with your eagerness!

Lord, I enjoy some of my activities—the fun stuff, mostly. I don't always love cleaning my room or clearing the table after we eat. Remind me every day that you enjoy watching me work, no matter how hard the task!

LOOKING FOR GOD

"When you come looking for me, you'll find me. Yes, when you get serious about finding me and want it more than anything else, I'll make sure you won't be disappointed. . . . I'll turn things around for you."
JEREMIAH 29:13–14 MSG

If you went on a scavenger hunt, looking for God, where do you think you would find Him? Is He hiding under the bed? Up on the rooftop? Is He behind the table or up on a mountaintop? Do you have to go far to find Him?

The truth is, God is as close as your heart. It's a fact! He's right there. When you ask Jesus to be your Lord and Savior, He comes to live inside of your heart and is always there when you need Him. So call out to Him today. But remember, there's no need to yell. He's so close, He can't help but hear your softest whisper.

It's time to get serious about hanging out with the Lord. Let Him know that you want Him more than anything else. Then when you draw near to Him (in prayer), He will meet you and change your situation. He will turn things around for you. And He'll do it all without ever leaving the center of your heart.

Dear Lord, thank You for residing in my heart. I love it that You're so near to me! I know You will never disappoint me.

THE IMAGE OF OUR DADDY

So God created man in his own image, in the image of God
created he him; male and female created he them.

GENESIS 1:27 KJV

. . . .

Has anyone ever told you that you have your mom's eyes? Or maybe some say, "You have your father's nose!" Truth is, you might look like your earthly parents, but you also look like your heavenly Father. He created you in His image.

It's fun to imagine what God looks like. We won't know for sure until we get to heaven, but one thing is clear—you are created in His image. So, does that mean God has red hair and freckles? Does it mean He wears tennis shoes? Does He like to go shopping and hang out with His friends after school?

Not exactly. To be created in the "image" of God means you look like Him on the inside. When you smile, it's *His* smile that's coming through. When you're sweet to others, it's *His* sweetness that they see. When you stop to give someone a helping hand, it's as if *His* hand is reaching out to that person.

We are all created in the image of our Daddy God. When people look at you, they see a shining reflection of Him. So the next time someone says, "Hey, you look like your dad!" just smile. They're right, you know.

. . . .

Lord, I love hearing that I take after You. It makes me wonder what
You look like! Someday I'll know for sure, but until then,
thank You for creating me in Your image, Father!

TRUSTING IN THE HARD TIMES

The LORD is my rock, my fortress and my deliverer; my God is my
rock, in whom I take refuge, my shield and the horn
of my salvation, my stronghold.

PSALM 18:2 NIV

Do you trust—totally depend on—anyone in your life? Perhaps your parents? Your friends? Yourself? Have you ever put your trust in someone and then gotten disappointed when she let you down by not doing what she said she would?

If the list of people you can count on is very small, don't worry. There is Someone you *can* totally trust, One who will never let you down. He will always be there for you, no matter what. He is the Lord, your rock, your fortress (strong place), and the One who will deliver you from (take you out of) scary places. You can place your trust in Him and not have to worry about being disappointed.

We all go through scary times, but walking through them with our trust in God helps so much! We don't have to panic because we know that He's got everything under control. So know that you can trust Him, girl. . .even when it's tough. You'll never be sorry.

Lord, I have to admit, I don't always trust. Sometimes my faith slips!
Show me how to keep on trusting, even when it's really hard.
I don't ever want to let go of Your hand!

WHiSTLE A HAPPY TuNE

O clap your hands, all ye people;
shout unto God with the voice of triumph.
PSALM 47:1 KJV

Do you like to work? Some people are workaholics! They dive right in and get the job done. Others move more slowly or need reminders from parents or teachers.

If you're not thrilled with the idea of working, working, working, listen up! There's a way to lighten the load as you work. Remember the old song the seven dwarves sang to Snow White? The one about whistling while you work? Singing a happy song like that seems to make everything easier. No kidding!

Are you having a hard time getting along with your brother or sister? Whistle a happy tune. Are you having an argument with a friend at school? Worried? Upset? Mad at Mom or Dad? Turn on some praise music! It will change your attitude in a hurry. Best of all, singing a song to Jesus turns your focus away from your work and troubles and onto your heavenly Father, who adores you. Your spirits can't help but be lifted as you sing out a song of praise.

Father, some days I'm not happy about having to clean my room and do the dishes. Other times, arguments with friends and family can make me really sad—and mad. Thank You for reminding me that singing a happy song (praising You) can change my attitude—about anything and everything.

Ain't no nobodies!

For you created my inmost being; you knit me together in my mother's womb. I praise you because I am fearfully and wonderfully made; your works are wonderful, I know that full well.

<small>PSALM 139:13–14 NIV</small>

Do you believe that God made you special? He did! He wouldn't take the time to create a nobody. He's all about creating somebodies! You're so special to Him and to the people around you. Sure, you don't always feel special (no one does), but you have to believe it anyway. Whenever you start to doubt it, get to the truth of the matter by reading and believing today's scripture!

Just in case you haven't figured out what makes you special, know this: You were uniquely created to be *you!* No one else. On top of that, you've been given special talents and gifts. And God's been planning all of this for a long time, even before you were born. When you were in your mom's tummy, God knew just exactly what you would look like, how special you would be. Way back then He started working on the blueprint (the plan) for how you would turn out.

If God went to this much trouble to make you so unique and talented, He must know what He's doing! And He says you're special, so you have to trust Him, even on days when you don't feel like it.

God, sometimes I don't feel very special. I look at my friends who are really pretty or the girls who make great grades and I feel like I don't measure up. Thank You, Father, for reminding me that I'm special in Your sight!

RUN THE RACE

Therefore, since we are surrounded by such a great cloud of witnesses, let us throw off everything that hinders and the sin that so easily entangles. And let us run with perseverance the race marked out fo us, fixing our eyes on Jesus, the pioneer and perfecter of faith.
HEBREWS 12:1–2 NIV

Do you like to run in races? Have you ever made it all the way to the finish line? If so, then you probably understand the verse above. Our lives are like a race. God has a finish line (heaven) and we keep running until we get there! The problem is, sometimes we get tired and want to quit. We think it's too hard to be a Christian. There are too many temptations. We just want to be like our friends—to do what we want when we want. But that would mean we've come to a standstill.

Here's the thing: this race is winnable, but you've got to keep running. You've also got to have a plan. . .a strategy. Before you start each day, do your daily "stretches" (reading your Bible and praying); then put one foot in front of the other.

Begin to see yourself as a winner of the race. God already sees you that way! Sure, you'll be tempted to stop, but whenever that happens, just pray and then dive back in with both feet, your eyes on the finish line.

◄ So start stretching! Get ready to run! Then get set and go!

Sometimes I get tired of running, Lord. When I'm exhausted, please help me see that You can give me the strength to keep going. I can win the race with Your hand in mine.

BEING A GIANT KILLER

David asked the men standing near him, "What will be done for the man who kills this Philistine and removes this disgrace from Israel? Who is this uncircumcised Philistine that he should defy the armies of the living God?"

1 SAMUEL 17:26 NIV

Have you ever read the story of David and Goliath? David, a little shepherd boy, killed the mighty (evil) giant, Goliath, with a slingshot and a stone. Wow. Brave kid, right? Did you know that God can give you the courage to kill giants too? Oh, they might not look like Goliath. They're not even real people. But they're giants just the same. Anything that tries to stop you from doing what God wants you to do could be considered your "Goliath."

What are some of the "giants" you need to kill? Jealousy? Anger? Bitterness? Lying? These are all huge enemies that can cause you problems if you don't deal with them. It's time to reach for your slingshot! Let God help you take aim at the big, bad giants and knock 'em down with His mighty power! You can't do it in your own strength, but God is right there, ready to do the fighting for you. It's time to face some giants, kiddo!

God, sometimes I look at the "giants" in my life—bad habits, sins, things I can't seem to stop doing—and wonder if I'll ever be able to slay them. You helped David take down Goliath, so I know, with Your help, I can slay the giants in my own life. Thank You, Lord!

MiRROR, MiRROR ON THE WALL

"Before I shaped you in the womb, I knew all about you.
Before you saw the light of day, I had holy plans for you."
JEREMIAH 1:5 MSG

Have you ever looked in a mirror and wished you could change something? Ever pretend to be someone else—someone who looked different and had different talents and abilities? If you were an actress upon a stage, your pretending to be someone you're not would be fun, wouldn't it? But in the real world, it's better to just be yourself. God made you. . .you! And He did it on purpose!

Think about it—the King of kings, your Daddy God, decided even before you were born just what you would look like. He specially selected the color of your hair, your skin, your eyes. . .everything! He decided how tall or short you would be, and dropped in some extra-special talents and abilities, just for fun! Your awesome Creator took great care in making all of these very important decisions.

When God looks at you, He loves what He sees! So the next time you look in the mirror and want to grumble, take the time to thank Him for making you. . .you!

Lord, sometimes when I see my reflection in the mirror I wish I could
change the way I look. It helps so much to know that You made
me exactly like I am, and You love me that way!

THE GIRL JESUS LOVES!

Then the disciple whom Jesus loved said to Peter,
"It is the Lord!" As soon as Simon Peter heard him say,
"It is the Lord," he wrapped his outer garment around him
(for he had taken it off) and jumped into the water.
JOHN 21:7 NIV

Did you ever stop to think about how much Jesus loves you? It's more than just a song you learned in church—"Jesus Loves Me, This I Know." When, in your heart and mind, you know He loves you, you don't have to worry when you make mistakes. Think about that for a minute. We all sin and fall short, don't we? But when we're absolutely, totally convinced that Jesus loves us, we don't have to worry that our mistakes will make Him *stop* loving us.

One of Jesus' disciples really knew how much he was loved. His name was John. He called himself "the disciple whom Jesus loved." Can you say that today? Can you say, "I'm the girl Jesus loves!" You are, you know. And He will never ever stop loving you, no matter what.

Oh Lord, I'm so glad that I'm a girl You can love. I've made mistakes, Father, but You go on forgiving me and loving me anyway. Thank You for that!

LEARNING TO LOVE

" 'Love the Lord your God with all your heart and with
all your soul and with all your mind and with all your strength.'
The second is this: 'Love your neighbor as yourself.' "

MARK 12:30–31 NIV

Some girls get excited when they think about growing up and falling in love. Others don't like the idea at all! Where do you stand?

Here's good news for you: you don't have to worry about it! Right now, the only "true love" you need to focus on is the Lord. The Bible says that *He* is your first love. *And* He's got the best plan for how you can love all sorts of other people too—even when you're young! So God wants you to:

1. Love Him more than anything. You may be saying, "Whoa! Seriously? More than my parents? My friends? My clothes? My video games?" Yep. Start by putting your love for your heavenly Father above every other thing. Love Him with all of your heart, soul, mind, and strength. That's a lot of love!

2. Love yourself. "It's okay to love myself?" Sure! If you don't love yourself, it's pretty hard to love others. You just have to remember not to put yourself first—above God. It's not all about you, after all. It's all about Him.

3. Love others as you love yourself. Put their needs above your own, even when it's hard. Remember that God loves others just as much as He loves you.

Dear Lord, when I think about growing up and falling in love, it's kind of scary! I'm so glad You're teaching me now what it really means to love others and to love You. Thank You, Father! You're my One True Love.

FOR SUCH A TIME AS THIS

"For if you remain silent at this time, relief and deliverance for the Jews will arise from another place, but you and your father's family will perish. And who knows but that you have come to your royal position for such a time as this?"

ESTHER 4:14 NIV

There's an amazing story in the Bible about a girl named Esther who became a queen at just the right time. She had to face some big challenges, but she trusted God, and her people (the Jews) were saved because of her faithfulness. She was young, but that didn't stop her! Oh, no! She allowed God to use her.

Did you ever think that you have the same faith power as Esther? You know, you too were born "for such a time as this." That means you were placed among the right "people"—your friends and family members—at the right time. It's true! When you pray for your family members (your brothers, sisters, parents, aunts, uncles, and so on) and friends, God is listening. Your prayers could be the doorway that leads them to a relationship with Jesus.

So don't stop praying, no matter what. Like Esther, your prayers are powerful! Keep on hoping, keep on trusting, just like she did. Who knows? Maybe all your "people" will end up loving God and living for Him!

Dear Lord, can You make me an Esther? I want to pray for my "people" and watch every one of them come to know You! Thank You that I was born "for such a time as this"!

ME, MYSELF, AND I?

"The second is this: 'You shall love your neighbor as yourself.'
There is no other commandment greater than these."

MARK 12:31 ESV

Have you ever met someone who's totally self-focused? All he ever talks about is himself or, as he calls it, "me, myself, and I." Every time you try to say something, he interrupts you and tells another story about something he's going through. This type of self-absorbed, "me"-focused person is tough to be around. He's missing out on caring more about others, isn't he? What a shame.

Why are so many people so focused on themselves, anyway? Why don't they notice that other people have needs too? One reason is that the enemy (the devil) has blinded them to God's plan. And they're not alone. The world is filled with people who don't seem to notice the needs of others.

You can be different. You can be "others" focused. You can see those around you who are hurting, hungry, and sick, and you can pray for them. Instead of always talking about yourself or worrying about your own needs, you can pay more attention to the ones all around you who need help.

Yes, you can be different. No more "me, myself, and I."

Dear Lord, I don't want to be "me" focused. Thank You for showing me that other people are going through stuff and need my love and my prayers.

PRIDE

Pride leads to disgrace,
but with humility comes wisdom.
PROVERBS 11:2 NLT

What does it mean to be prideful? Is pride a bad thing? Some people are proud of their local football or baseball team. They're proud of their children, proud of their home, and proud of a host of other things. Is this wrong? Not necessarily.

But pride does slip us up when we start to think we're better than others (prettier, smarter, more talented, and so on). *That* kind of pride is definitely not good. God wants us to walk humbly around our friends. That means we are not to think we're better than they are. We are to recognize their talents and their gifts, and encourage them by making them feel good about themselves. We are not to compare ourselves to them, either. None of this "I'm better than you are!" stuff. No way.

The next time you feel like you're better than someone else...watch out! The Lord isn't happy with that kind of puffed-up attitude! So lay down that pride, girl! Get rid of it. Begin to focus more on others and less on yourself. Doing so will please God's heart!

Lord, sometimes I get a little prideful. I think I'm better than others.
Please remind me that this attitude doesn't please You.
Then help me get rid of my pride.

THE BEST WAY TO DRESS

And to all these things, you must add love. Love holds everything and everybody together and makes all these good things perfect.
COLOSSIANS 3:14 NLV

Have you ever had one of those mornings when you just couldn't decide what to wear? Maybe you picked out one outfit, put it on, then decided to wear something else. Once you were re-dressed and looked in the mirror, you weren't happy with *that* outfit, either. Before long everything ended up in a pile on the floor, and you still weren't sure what looked best. Decisions, decisions!

What you wear is important to you, but one item in your wardrobe is especially important to God. Reach way back into your closet or into your drawer and pull out. . .love! Love is like a garment. It's something you put on. You can wear it all day long. Oh, it's not made of fabric and thread. No way. It's not even something people can see with their eyes. But it's probably the most important garment you can wear. So slip it over each shoulder. Wrap it around your heart. There! Doesn't that feel nice? It's by far the most attractive thing you can put on!

Seem a little silly? It's not. Wear love like you would wear a warm, fuzzy jacket. Let it surround you on every side so that when you bump into people—and you surely will—God and His love will rub off on them too! Slip it over your head, like a winter cap, so that your thoughts are always *His* thoughts.

Love—now *that's* one attractive outfit!

Father, thank You for reminding me that the most important item
I can wear is Your love. May I never forget to put it on!

DO NOT DENY

Now Simon Peter stood and warmed himself. Therefore they said
to him, "You are not also one of His disciples, are you?"
He denied it and said, "I am not!"
JOHN 18:25 NKJV

There's a really sad story in the New Testament. It's about one of Jesus' disciples—a man named Peter. He loved Jesus so much. But when things got scary, Peter made a very bad decision—he decided to deny that he knew Jesus. To *deny* something means to claim it isn't true, even if it is. For example, let's say you broke one of your mom's fancy china plates and she asked if you did it. If you said, "No," you would be denying it.

To deny *Jesus* is to tell your friends, "I never knew Him." Can you believe Peter would do that? Well, sometimes we do the same thing without even realizing it. We give our hearts to Jesus and then get wrapped up in what we want to do. Our friends ask us to do something we know we shouldn't do. And we go along with them, totally forgetting about our promises to live for Jesus. We're not denying Him on purpose, of course, but we're still breaking His heart by forgetting our promises. We have to make up our minds never to deny Him. Instead, we need to live for Him every day!

Father, I don't ever want to deny You! May I always remember
my promise to walk with You every day of my life!

DON'T FORGET THE LESSON!

Stick with what you learned and believed,
sure of the integrity of your teachers.
2 TIMOTHY 3:14 MSG

Think about all of the things you've learned from your parents, Sunday school teachers, and the other believing adults in your life. They have such a blast teaching you about the Bible, and you're a great student! God loves it when you remember what you've learned, but let's face it. . .it's easy to walk away and forget the lesson, isn't it?

Here's an example: You're in your Sunday school class and your teacher tells you all about the fruits of the Spirit. She explains that God wants you to be good, kind, gentle, faithful, and so on. You leave the class feeling really good about what you've learned. Then, a few days later, you get in a fight with your little sister and treat her badly, forgetting all about the lesson.

Here's the thing: if we want to really grow up in Christ, we need to stick with what we have learned. We can't be patient one minute then impatient the next. We can't be kind one day then mean-spirited the next. To make sure the lesson really sticks, we've got to go to God in prayer and ask Him for help to go on doing the right thing, no matter what!

Dear Lord, I want to learn my lesson and learn it well! I don't want to walk away and forget. Please let all of Your lessons stick to me like glue!

GIVING YOUR BEST

Concentrate on doing your best for God, work you won't be ashamed of, laying out the truth plain and simple.

2 TIMOTHY 2:15 MSG

God wants His kids to do their best for Him. That doesn't mean you "sort of" do what He tells you to. Instead, you go all the way! He loves it when you step it up. If you're looking for some great ways to do that, here are some suggestions: Give God your very best attitude (even when it's really hard)! Give Him your best time of day. (Don't wait until you're too tired to pray and read your Bible.) Give an offering at church. (Putting money in the offering plate is a great way to show that you're dedicated to God.) Give Him your best behavior when you're around your parents, your teachers, and your friends.

There are dozens of other ways you can give your best! For example, you could collect canned goods to donate to your church's food pantry. Make a game of it! Challenge other churchgoers to promise to match what you give on your own! Or maybe you could donate clothing or blankets to help the homeless in winter. There are a zillion ways to help out! Be willing to give your talents and treasures. Best of all, give your heavenly Father your very best!

Dear Lord, I want to step it up! I want to give You my very best.
Help me to do that every day of my life!

FROM DARKNESS TO LIGHT

If anyone claims, "I am living in the light," but hates a Christian brother
or sister, that person is still living in darkness. Anyone who loves another
brother or sister is living in the light and does not cause others to stumble.

1 JOHN 2:9–10 NLT

How do you feel when you're in the dark, when it's so dark that you can't see anything at all? Imagine you're in your bedroom late at night and the light is off. You suddenly realize you forgot to do something, so you get out of bed and tiptoe across the dark room. Along the way, you run into something and hurt yourself. Ouch! Being in the dark isn't just about not being able to see properly—it's also dangerous!

Why are you more likely to hurt yourself when the lights are out? Because your eyes don't totally adjust to the darkness. Your vision is limited. You can't see the details. There's nothing there to guide you. Because you can't see, you stumble into things, which can cause you pain!

It's the same in your Christian life. When the light is turned on, you can see where you're going. You no longer stumble—nor trip others up. And what is the switch that turns on the light? It's love! You've got to turn it on—whether you're at school, with your friends, at the mall, or just hanging out at home with your brothers and sisters. Love is the switch that lights the way and keeps you—and others—from tripping up.

God, I don't want to stumble around in the dark. Open my eyes
so that I can clearly see the road You want to lead me down.

PRESS ON!

*I press toward the goal for the prize of the
upward call of God in Christ Jesus.*
PHILIPPIANS 3:14 NKJV

Some people have a hard time getting over things. They get stuck on what happened yesterday. Maybe you're the same way. You can't seem to forgive your friend for what she said about you. Or maybe you can't seem to get over how you felt when your friends wouldn't hang out with you. Yesterdays can be hurtful, for sure. That's why God wants you to live in today.

How do you live in today and not the past? Check out the scripture above. Press toward the goal. When you're in a race, you'll be looking ahead, not backward. It's the same with life. Don't look back to yesterday. Forgive. And move on.

The problems of yesterday might have been big, but they are behind you now. To keep the proper perspective, look ahead. Stay focused! There's a race to be won, and you don't want to trip and fall because you were looking backward instead of forward!

Lord, thank You for reminding me that I always need to look forward,
not backward. I choose to forgive the people who hurt me yesterday.
I choose to live in today only, with Your hand in mine!

GOD IS OMNISCIENT (A REAL KNOW-It-ALL!)

Great is our Lord, and great in power.
His understanding has no end.
PSALM 147:5 NLV

- -

How big is your God? Do you think He's bigger than the problems you face at school? Bigger than the friendships that aren't working out? Bigger than your grandmother's illness?

Isn't it amazing to think that God is all-knowing? He's got it all figured out—yesterday, today, and tomorrow. Because of this, we can trust Him with every single thing we go through in this life, from the little things to the huge things! There's no better way to live than handing over the reins to our omniscient God!

God doesn't shrink. He doesn't get smaller when you're going through tough stuff. He's enormous! Powerful! When you think about Him that way, you can see it's pointless to worry. Your omniscient God—He's got this!

- -

Dear Lord, sometimes I go through bad stuff. I get scared. I forget how
powerful You are! You created the world in just a few days. I'm sure
You can take care of all my problems without any trouble at all!

I'm a Mess!

For I am convinced that neither death nor life, neither angels nor demons,
neither the present nor the future, nor any powers, neither height nor
depth, nor anything else in all creation, will be able to separate
us from the love of God that is in Christ Jesus our Lord.

ROMANS 8:38–39 NIV

Have you ever messed up so badly that you wondered if your parents (or friends) could go on loving you? Have you ever woken up feeling grumpy or hard to get along with and become a terror to be around? Sure. We all have days like that. We all go through those times.

Here's the thing about human beings (and not just kids): we mess up. A lot. We say we love people; then we don't behave like it. We act like we're best friends with someone one day then move on to a new best friend the next. In other words, we're a mess that sometimes messes up!

Here's what saves us: God doesn't change His mind. When He says He loves us, He means it. He loves us—forever and always! And there's nothing you can do to change that. Nothing. On your best day, He's right there, loving you. On your worst day, He's right there, still loving you. Absolutely nothing can separate you from the love of God that is in Christ Jesus!

Father, it's such a relief to hear that my messes don't mess up Your
plan to go on loving me! Thank You for always being there
for me, even when I'm having a terrible day.

38

LiFE IS A PUZZLE

"For I know the plans I have for you, declares the LORD, plans for
welfare and not for evil, to give you a future and a hope."
JEREMIAH 29:11 ESV

Sometimes life is like a jigsaw puzzle. And we get frustrated because we can't see the whole picture. Has that ever happened to you while doing a puzzle? You think you've got it all figured out, but then the pieces don't fit? Or you can't find the exact one you need at the exact time you need it? But that's half the adventure! If we could see it all at once, it would take all the joy, fun, excitement, and gratefulness out of the journey. In other words, life would be pretty boring!

Here's some great news: God has all the pieces in His hand! He's got a great plan for your life, and He knows just what you need when you need it. You have to trust that no matter where you go, no matter what you do, He's going to put the next piece of the puzzle in at just the right time and guide you to your next step.

Learning to trust God with the puzzle pieces of your life is a challenge at times, but it's so worth it! So relax. Let go, and let God put the pieces together in His time and His way. Trust Him with the whole picture.

God, I'm so glad that You hold all of the puzzle pieces! I don't really
know what's going to happen next, but You do! I'm so
grateful. Teach me to trust as I wait on You.

I WiLL BE GLAD

I will be glad and rejoice in you; I will sing the
praises of your name, O Most High.

PSALM 9:2 NIV

. . . .

What does it mean to be glad in the Lord? Does it mean you're always laughing and singing? No. It means you've placed your trust in Him and have the peace that comes when you remove your hands from the situation. Gladness comes when you let go—and let God!

Did you know that some days you have to choose to be glad? It's true! You won't feel like it. You might feel like being grumpy or sour. You might feel like staying in bed all day, pulling the covers over your head! But God wants you to wake up, bounce out of bed, and enjoy your day with a big smile on your face. Be glad! Celebrate!

But how do you go from grumpy to glad? Start by singing praises to God. When you raise your voice in song, all of your problems go away for that moment. You're only focused on Him. So rejoice and be glad! It's a choice you should—and can—always make.

. . . .

Dear Lord, today I choose joy. I will be glad, no matter what I'm going
through. I ask that You put a song of praise in my heart so that
I can see past my problems and focus on You!

PRAISE YOUR WAY THROUGH

Sing to him, sing praise to him; tell of all his wonderful acts.

1 CHRONICLES 16:9 NIV

There's an awesome story in the Bible about a man named Jehoshaphat who was about to go to war against his enemies (see 2 Chronicles 20). Before he set off for battle, God said: "Don't worry, Jehoshaphat! I've got this! You won't even have to fight. I'll do the fighting for you!" Cool, right?

Jehoshaphat, knowing God had the victory in hand, sent the Levites (the praise and worship guys) to the front of the battle. They lifted their voices in praise, and guess what? The battle was won! Wow!

The same thing is true in our lives. Whenever we face battles or challenges (and we all do), we need to have the courage of Jehoshaphat, knowing that God will fight the battle for us. We also have to sing praises, even before the battle is won. This elevates our courage and reminds us that God is in control. If you're facing a challenge today, try praising your way through!

Dear Lord, thank You for the reminder that You fight my battles for me.
Sometimes I feel weak, but You are strong! When I praise You,
I remember that You are in control, not me!

LOVE. . .AND OBEY

"If you love me, keep my commands."

JOHN 14:15 NIV

Jesus told His disciples, "If you love me, keep my commands." Love and obedience go hand-in-hand. So the next time you say, "I love you," to your mom, it might be a good idea to follow it up with obedience to her, perhaps by doing what she's already told you to do. Or the next time a grandparent says, "I love you, honey," and you respond with, "I love you too!" remember those words carry a lot of meaning and that with those words should come actions to prove it!

Question: How do you show God that you love Him? Answer: Obey! Yes, that's it. Obey. You may be asking, "So is love all about obedience? Isn't there more to it?" Sure. To love someone means you're completely dedicated to her, that you will care for her—always and in all ways. That means you will stick with that TLC (Tender Loving Care), even when it's hard. Let's face it, it's not always easy to obey or to love everyone. Some people are tough!

If you love, you obey. If you love, treat others better than yourself. If you love, make your bed. If you love, do your homework. If you love. . .well, you get the idea. Obedience isn't always easy, but it's always right.

Father, I don't always like to obey. Sometimes I just like to get
my own way. Thank You for the reminder that love means
obedience. Help me to obey, no matter what!

42

THE POPULARITY CONTEST

What if a man comes into your church wearing a gold ring and good clothes?
And at the same time a poor man comes wearing old clothes. What if you
show respect to the man in good clothes and say, "Come and sit in this good
place"? But if you say to the poor man, "Stand up over there," or "Sit on the
floor by my feet," are you not thinking that one is more important
than the other? This kind of thinking is sinful.

JAMES 2:2–4 NLV

Are you picky when it comes to selecting your friends? Do you choose only the popular girls to hang out with, the ones in the "in" crowd? If so, you might want to think twice!

God loves all of His daughters equally—from the most popular to the least. From the best dressed to the one in rags. From the teacher's pet to the girl who keeps getting into trouble in class. God doesn't play favorites. (He just loves you so much that it feels like you're His favorite!) He adores girls of every size, shape, and color.

God doesn't want you to play favorites, either. It's hard, but so important not to! We need to remember this whenever we're tempted to hang out with someone just because she seems to be popular or cool. Maybe the Lord wants you to spend a little time with the girl on the bus who has no friends. You know the one. . . she gets made fun of a lot. Get to know her, and see what God does.

Lord, please help me be a better friend! I don't want to judge others
or be a picky girl. Remind me that You love us all equally.

THE LIGHT SIDE

Our hope comes from God. May He fill you with joy and peace because of your trust in Him. May your hope grow stronger by the power of the Holy Spirit.

ROMANS 15:13 NLV

Don't you love hanging out with friends who have a great sense of humor? They know how to laugh, and how to make you laugh too! Their lighthearted attitude is so much fun. They always lift the spirits of others.

Here's a fun idea: Why not *be* that lighthearted person? Why not lift the spirits of others and keep them smiling even when they're going through tough stuff. When you go out of your way to bring joy to others, you bring joy to yourself too! That's always fun.

Wondering where all of this joy comes from? From God, of course! If you ask Him to fill you up, He will do it. Then you will spill out on others and they will soon forget about their troubles. So fill up your joy tank today, and then overflow on everyone you meet!

Father, I'm so excited that I can be a joy spiller! I ask that You fill me up, up, up to the tippy-top so that I can spill over onto others who are having a hard day.

"No Fair!"

Do everything without grumbling or arguing, so that you may become blameless and pure, "children of God without fault in a warped and crooked generation." Then you will shine among them like stars in the sky as you hold firmly to the word of life. And then I will be able to boast on the day of Christ that I did not run or labor in vain.

PHILIPPIANS 2:14–16 NIV

Imagine this: You're exhausted! Tired after a super long day at school. You're just chilling. Resting. Playing a video game. Reading a book. Talking to a friend on the phone. Then you hear those words. . .you know the ones! It's your mom's voice, and she needs you to do the dishes. Or help take care of your little sister. Or clean up your bedroom. Ugh!

You want to holler, "But I don't feel like it! I did all of that yesterday. Puh-*leeze* ask someone else. It's always my turn." Maybe you even say something like, "No fair, Mom!"

Here's the problem with the no-fair attitude: Jesus tells us not to have it. In fact, He says that we're to do everything without complaining. Sounds impossible, but we're supposed to try anyway! Mumbling and grumbling are out. A grateful heart is in. To please God, we have to learn to respond the way He wants us to. It isn't always easy, but He honors a cheerful, obedient daughter!

Father, sometimes it's so hard to do things without complaining. Today I ask that You help me respond in a way that brings joy to Your heart!

WALK BY FAITH

For we walk by faith, not by sight.
2 CORINTHIANS 5:7 KJV

. . . .

There's an amazing story in the Old Testament about a man named Noah who heard God's voice. The Lord told him to build a huge boat and to load it up with animals. . .lots and lots of animals. Why? Because God was going to send a huge flood, and He wanted Noah, his family, and the animals to be safe. It's a good thing Noah listened to God. If he hadn't, he and his wife and children would have drowned! (And all of those animals too!)

It's so important to listen for God's voice. He still speaks, you know. He speaks to the heart. That little "feeling" you get, telling you that you should help someone in need? That's the Lord! That little nudging you get, prompting you to obey when you don't feel like it? That's God's voice too! He's always talking—and hoping we will listen up!

When you pray, it's important to speak to God, but it's also very important to listen. He has a lot He wants to say to you. Maybe He's speaking right now. Shh! Can you hear Him?

. . . .

Lord, sometimes I forget that You like to talk to me.
Speak to my heart, Father. Show me what to do. I am listening!

HOPES AND DREAMS

Be strong. Be strong in heart, all you who hope in the Lord.
PSALM 31:24 NLV

Have you ever wished for something—really, really wished for it? Maybe you were so hopeful that your dream or wish would come true that you could hardly think of anything else.

Life is filled with wishes and dreams. There's so much to look forward to as you grow and grow and grow! It's so much fun to think about what you'll be like when you get older. Maybe you'll be a brilliant scientist who discovers the cure to a terrible illness. Maybe you'll be president of the United States! Maybe you will be a mom and one of your children will be a missionary who leads thousands to Christ. The possibilities are endless.

Don't ever give up on your hopes and dreams, even if they seem impossible. Sometimes God lays those things on your heart for a reason.

Dear Lord, I'm such a dreamer sometimes! When I grow up,
I want my life to be amazing! Thank You for giving me
hopes and dreams. I trust You with my future, Father.

CREATED TO WORSHIP!

I called to the LORD, who is worthy of praise, and
I have been saved from my enemies.

PSALM 18:3 NIV

People can be a lot of trouble! Did you ever wonder why God created them in the first place? He could have settled for living with the birds and the fish and the other animals. They're much more obedient. Why create human beings?

The Bible says that we were created to worship God. If we don't praise Him, the rocks will begin to shout out praises to the King of kings. (Can you imagine the rocks bursting out in joyful song?) We don't want the rocks to have to do that! We're going to be praising Him for all eternity, so why not start practicing now?

God is worthy to be praised! He's so amazing and awesome. He created the whole world—just by speaking it into existence. He sent His Son to die on the cross—proving His love for us, once and for all. Yes, God truly loves us, and that alone makes Him worthy!

A daughter of the King can't say enough good things about her Father. Why, she brags on Him all day long! She sings His praises to everyone who will listen. So let a song of praise fill your heart today. If you don't...the rocks will surely begin to shout!

Lord, I love to brag on You! It's easy to tell other people about all of the amazing things You do. How exciting, to know that I'm going to go on praising You forever...and ever...and ever!

CHILDREN OF GOD

See what great love the Father has lavished on us,
that we should be called children of God!
And that is what we are!

1 JOHN 3:1 NIV

I know, I know! Sometimes it's no fun being called a child. Maybe you wish you were not so young. Or maybe you wish you were *all* grown up. Those days are coming, for sure! For now, you can't help thinking that being called a little kid makes you sound so. . .babyish, right?

Maybe not. The Bible teaches that people who want to know God, to really know Him, should be like little kids, innocent and pure, ready to believe what they are told. When you're really little, you trust. You love. You don't doubt. You're not worried about what others think or say.

The Bible says that we are all children of God. . .and that's a good thing! We are His kids. There's something pretty special about being in His family. He loves us like the best daddy in the world. He takes care of us, protects us, and helps us through rough times.

Yes, sometimes it's okay to be a kid, especially with a Father like God!

Daddy God. . .I love calling You that! I don't usually like
to be called a child, but I love being called Your child.
Thank You for adopting me and naming me as Your own!

WATCH THAT TEMPER, GIRL!

But now also put these things out of your life:
anger, bad temper, doing or saying things to hurt others,
and using evil words when you talk.
COLOSSIANS 3:8 NCV

Oooh, sometimes we get so mad we just want to boil over! Imagine this: Your kid sister comes into your room and "borrows" your video game—or maybe even your favorite T-shirt—without asking! Then she loses it. Loses it! You've got a right to be mad, don't you? Surely God won't be upset if you give her a piece of your mind, telling her just what you think about her and what she's done.

Wrong. God doesn't want you to pitch a fit or throw a temper tantrum, even if you feel like you have a right to. Because you're a child of the King, He wants you to react the way He would react. The scripture above says that He wants you to put anger and hurtful words out of your life.

So how do you do that? How do you get rid of your anger? First, you need to pray about it. Give it to God. Tell Him that you don't want it anymore. Then every time you start to get mad, take a deep breath. . .and poof! Your anger will disappear!

Lord, please help me with my temper! Sometimes I totally lose it,
Lord. I don't mean to, but I do. I don't want to be known as a girl
who struggles with her temper, so I'm counting on You to help me!

GOD IS MOST IMPORTANT!

And God spoke all these words: "I am the LORD your God,
who brought you out of Egypt, out of the land of slavery.
You shall have no other gods before me."

EXODUS 20:1–3 NIV

. . . .

There once lived a really great man named Moses. You can read all about him in the Bible. He led his people out of Egypt to the Promised Land. Along the way, he came to a mountain. He climbed the mountain, and God gave him special commandments (rules) to give to the people. The very first commandment was "You shall have no other gods before me."

I'm sure Moses had a lot to think about when he heard those words. We have a lot to think about too! Like Moses, we have to be really careful not to make anything more important than our relationship with God. "No other gods" means nothing can mean more to us than He does. Not our toys. Not our friends. Not our entertainment. Not even our families. The most important thing has to be our relationship with God.

Is there anything in your life that's become too important? If so, ask God to forgive you, then put Him back in the most important place once again. God will bless you when you honor Him!

. . . .

Lord, sometimes I forget to put You first. Please keep reminding me that
You are the most important thing, above anything and anyone else!

COPYCAT!

Dear friend, do not imitate what is evil but what is good. Anyone who does what is good is from God. Anyone who does what is evil has not seen God.

3 JOHN 1:11 NIV

. . . .

Some girls are copycats. That's because they aren't happy just being themselves. Have you ever noticed them—girls dressing alike so they can feel like part of the crowd or talking alike so they will fit in?

Girls do like to imitate one another, don't they? They usually copy other girls—the ones they want to be like or the ones they want to like them. But in God's book, if you're going to be a copycat, you are to do it His way. He wants you to imitate Him! We are to be (and act) more like God, and there are so many ways to do that!

How do you imitate God? Start by reading the Gospels (Matthew, Mark, Luke, and John) to see what Jesus did—then go around copying what He did. For example, He was kind to the people most others were not kind to. (Can you do that?) He didn't treat one person better than another. (No playing favorites!) He cared for the sick, hurting, needy, and poor. (Can you do something for those people?)

If you want to imitate Jesus, be a good-deed doer! Then you'll be a great copycat!

. . . .

Lord, I don't mind copycatting You! I want to be more like You!
Remind me every day that You are the only One I should be copying!

YOUR SPECIAL TALENTS

For this reason, I ask you to keep using the gift God gave you.
It came to you when I laid my hands on you
and prayed that God would use you.
2 TIMOTHY 1:6 NLV

Did you know that God has given you special talents? It's true. You might not realize it, but you've been given many unique gifts. Maybe you can sing or play an instrument. Perhaps you enjoy acting or dancing—and love to perform on "the big stage." Maybe you prefer to scribble down your thoughts in your journal or write funny little poems to make people smile.

Remember, all of these abilities come from your heavenly Father, and He wants you to stir them up! Keep practicing. . .keep working at them! And while you're doing this, don't compare yourself to others. So what if someone else is a little better at something than you are? The Lord gave your friends gifts too, and He wants them to be used! All of His children are uniquely created, and it's such a blast to watch our talents grow!

The King of kings took the time to give you these very special gifts! Unwrap each one and use it to His glory!

Lord, thank You for blessing me with special gifts. I want to use them for You! Show me how I can do that and bring glory to Your name!

OH ME, OH MY!

I want to do what is good, but I don't. I don't want to do what is wrong,
but I do it anyway. But if I do what I don't want to do, I am not really
the one doing wrong; it is sin living in me that does it.

ROMANS 7:19–20 NLT

. . . .

Did you know that doing the right thing is usually not easy? In fact, sometimes doing the right thing is the hardest thing of all!

Here's a good example: Imagine your friend spreads a nasty rumor about you, one that's not true. You want to do the wrong thing—be mad at her. Fight back by telling people a story about her. Get others as mad at her as you are. But God, your heavenly Father, whispers in your ear: "Do the right thing. Forgive her."

"Forgive her? Are you kidding? After what she did to me?"

"Yes, forgive her. That's what a daughter of the King does. She turns the other cheek."

And so you swallow hard. . .and pray. You do the one thing that's hardest to do: you forgive your friend for hurting you. And you pray that God heals your broken friendship. In the end, your friend realizes how badly she's hurt you and asks for your forgiveness. You are able to be her friend once again, not because she asked, but because you had already forgiven her. God is happy and you are too!

See? Everyone wins when you make good choices. Sure, doing the right thing isn't always easy, but doing the right thing is *always* right.

. . . .

Lord, the next time I'm tempted to do the wrong thing, please stop me in my tracks! Help me do what's right, Father, even if it's very, very hard!

WORLD CHANGERS

*And [Jesus] said to [the disciples], "Go into all the world
and preach the gospel to every creature."*

MARK 16:15 NKJV

. . . .

What does it mean to "go into all the world" to share the Gospel? Does it mean you have to travel to the seven continents to tell people you've never met about Jesus? Not necessarily. Your "world" could be as close as your neighborhood or your own family! It could be your school or your local swimming pool. When you make up your mind to "go into all the world," you're telling God, "I want to be a world changer!"

World changers are those who aren't afraid to do things that make them uncomfortable. They don't just wade in the shallow end of the pool. They jump in the deep end. In other words, they go all out for God. They want to make a difference in their world. Their greatest prayer is to tell others about Jesus. They take the words of today's scripture very seriously.

Making a difference can be scary at times, but how wonderful to be used by God in new and exciting ways! When you tell Him that you want to be a world changer, He will give you the courage you need to win others to Him. This won't happen unless you get alone with Him and pray first. Ask Him to show you what to do. Once He shows You how to change the world, watch out! It's going to be a blast!

. . . .

Lord, I can't wait to change my world for You! Show me how to start!
I want to "go into all the world" and let other people
know just how much You love them.

FEAR. . .OR FAITH?

The LORD is my light and my salvation—whom shall I fear?
The LORD is the stronghold of my life—of whom shall I be afraid?
PSALM 27:1 NIV

Have you ever seen those commercials for spot remover—the handy-dandy stuff that's guaranteed to get even the toughest stains out? It seems to work like magic (at least through the TV screen). Wow!

Do you wish you had a "fear remover," something you could use to wash away all of your worries and fears in a hurry? Well, guess what? You do!

When you put your trust in God, you've got nothing to be afraid of. Scared of the dark? Fear, be gone! Scared of school? Fear, be gone! Scared of failing or being embarrassed around others? Fear, be gone—in Jesus' name!

God never intended for His kids to live in fear. In fact, faith is the opposite of fear. So the next time you start to get afraid, remember, God is your light and your salvation. Just look at that thing you're scared of and speak these words: "Fear, be gone—in Jesus' name!"

Lord, I'm so glad that I don't have to be afraid. Whew!
What a relief, Father. You send fear away in a hurry. I'm so grateful.

CONTENTMENT

A God-like life gives us much when we are happy for what we have.
We came into this world with nothing. For sure, when we die, we will
take nothing with us. If we have food and clothing, let us be happy.

1 Timothy 6:6–8 nlv

Have you ever heard the word *contentment*? It's a big word with an even bigger meaning. To be content means you're satisfied with what you have. You're not always wanting more. If you're content with your clothes, your toys, your video games, you're not always begging your parents to buy, buy, buy more stuff.

Being content is about more than stuff, though. To be really content means you're okay on the inside, even when things are hard on the outside. When you're going through hard times and life doesn't make any sense, you can trust that God is taking care of things. When you trust Him, you can be satisfied that everything is going to end up okay.

A girl who is content rests her head on the pillow at night and sleeps like a baby because she knows the Lord is in control. Are you a contented girl? If not, ask God to show you how you can be content in Him.

Lord, I want to be content. Help me to be satisfied with the things I have,
not always begging for more. And even when life is hard, help me to
remain content by trusting that You are working everything out.

GiViNG

"In everything I did, I showed you that by this kind of hard work we must help the weak, remembering the words the Lord Jesus himself said: 'It is more blessed to give than to receive.'"

ACTS 20:35 NIV

According to the Bible verse above, it's better to give than to receive. Amazing, right? Oh, receiving stuff is lots of fun, of course. Opening presents on Christmas day. Getting birthday gifts. Receiving money from your grandmother or aunt. It's a blast. No denying that! But why not spend a little time giving to others. Test it out and see which feels better—giving or receiving. You might just learn a thing or two!

Here are some ways you can give: Make a card for the elderly woman who lives on your street. Buy some bottled water or canned foods to give to the homeless or a local food pantry. Give away the clothes you've outgrown to someone who needs them. Save your money and support a child in another country.

There are all sorts of ways you can give. And you will feel so amazing when you do. It really is better to give than to receive!

Lord, I have to confess that I love getting things. . .sometimes more than I love giving. Make me more generous, Father! Make me a cheerful giver!

CREATION

*Even before he made the world, God loved us and chose us
in Christ to be holy and without fault in his eyes.*

EPHESIANS 1:4 NLT

. . . .

When you "create" something, it means you make something out of nothing. Think about that for a moment. Have you ever really created anything? Probably not! Everything we make is made out of something else.

Here's an example: When your mom wants to bake a pie, she uses ingredients like flour, eggs, shortening, and other foods. Sure, she bakes up a tasty pie, but she started with things that already existed. When God created the heavens and the earth, He took nothing and turned it into something. Pretty cool, right? He *truly* created! And He didn't stop with the heavens and the earth. He filled the earth with rivers and mountains, animals and fish, and lots more! How awesome!

Yes, we serve a very creative God who took great care in all of the things He made. His finest creation of all was us—His people. We're more important to Him than any of the animals, the trees, the oceans, or anything else. When He made us, He breathed His Spirit into us and created us in His image. Each one of us—including you—is very, very special to our Creator!

. . . .

Lord, I love that You took nothing and turned it into something. Wow!
It's so cool to think about that. Thank You for taking the time to create
the world. . .and thank You for taking the time to create me!

JUST A LITTLE BIT OF KINDNESS

If your enemy is hungry, give him food to eat;
if he is thirsty, give him water to drink.
PROVERBS 25:21 NIV

What would you do if your best friend suddenly decided she didn't want to be your friend anymore? What if your other friends did the same thing and you didn't know why? This sort of thing happens all the time, but not just to kids. It happens to grown-ups too, and it can be hurtful. People who start out as friends sometimes end up as enemies. In fact, things can get pretty ugly.

Did you know that it breaks God's heart when people don't get along? It's true. He wants His kids to love one another. But how is that possible, especially if people are mean to you? What can you do to make things better?

Instead of getting mad or even, why not try a little kindness? The Bible says we should not return evil for evil. Experience will show that it doesn't help to treat the other person badly. In fact, it just makes things worse!

This might sound crazy, but the next time a girlfriend treats you badly, do something nice for her. Send her a pretty card or give her a small gift, maybe something that means a lot to you. Just watch and see if a little kindness doesn't go a long, long way in making things better!

Lord, my feelings get so hurt sometimes. I don't know why some people don't want to be my friend. Thank You for being the best friend of all, one who will never leave me. Show me how to respond to others with kindness.

Running from God

But Jonah ran away from the Lord and headed for Tarshish. He went down to Joppa, where he found a ship bound for that port. After paying the fare, he went aboard and sailed for Tarshish to flee from the Lord.

JONAH 1:3 NIV

Have you ever had to do something so big, so scary, that you just wanted to run in the opposite direction? If so, then you should read the story of Jonah! God asked Jonah to do something really hard and Jonah was terrified, so he ran away! But God, in His own special way, got Jonah's attention again.

Jonah, who had tried to sail away from God, was thrown off a big ship and swallowed by a giant fish. (Icky!) He stayed inside the fish for three days but finally got out. He had a lot of repenting to do. That means he had to tell God that he was sorry he had run away in the first place.

What can we learn from Jonah's story? Don't run from God's plans for your life. Sure, you will have to do hard things sometimes. You'll be scared. But trust God to give you the courage to do what needs to be done. Don't run—or sail—away. Face the big stuff head-on!

Lord, sometimes I have to do hard things, things I don't want
to do. I want to turn and run, but I don't want to be a Jonah!
Please give me the courage to do what You ask me to do.

FACING YOUR GIANTS

Goliath, a Philistine champion from Gath, came out of the Philistine ranks to face the forces of Israel. He was over nine feet tall!

1 SAMUEL 17:4 NLT

Have you ever heard the word *obstacle*? An obstacle is something that gets in your way. For instance, if you were running a race and a huge mountain appeared in front of you, that would be a big obstacle!

There's a story in the Bible about a little shepherd boy named David who came across a great big obstacle—a giant named Goliath! He faced his obstacle and then knocked him down with one stone and a slingshot. Wow! There's something pretty fabulous about working up the courage to stand strong, even when everything is against you.

So what obstacles do you face? Bad grades? A situation at home with your parents? A problem with a friend? Maybe it seems huge, but it's really not. Just ask God to give you the courage of David the shepherd boy. With God's help, all of the "big" things you come up against can be gone in the blink of an eye. So get out your slingshot! Get ready to take your giants down!

Lord, sometimes I face big obstacles. They seem huge to me!
I can't climb over them, I can't move them, I have to reach
for my slingshot! Help me have the faith of David so that
I can keep going, even when things get hard!

REJECTING REJECTION

*"If the world hates you, you know it hated
Me before it hated you."*

JOHN 15:18 NLV

Do you know what it means to be rejected? It means that people don't want anything to do with you. (Ouch!) They don't want to spend time with you or hang out with you.

We all face rejection. It's tough. We think we're accepted by our friends, but then they say, "Go away. We don't want to be your friends anymore." Why do they do this? Who knows! People reject others for different reasons, most of which are just plain silly or prideful.

Do you want some fabulous advice for dealing with rejection? Reject it! Let it go. Don't feel sorry for yourself. Just forgive those who hurt you and move on. The very best thing you can do is this: make up your mind not to reject others even when they reject you. Accept them. Love them.

Why should we do this? Because we will never win others to the Lord if we reject them. We need to make everyone feel loved and accepted. When we do this, we are showing them God's love. So reject rejection! Get rid of it. Love everyone, and God will bless you.

Father, it hurts my feelings when people reject me.
I don't like it. Help me to forgive and to accept
all people so that I can show them Your love.

PRACTICE, PRACTICE, PRACTICE!

God is light, and there is no darkness in him at all.
So we are lying if we say we have fellowship with God but go
on living in spiritual darkness; we are not practicing the truth.

1 John 1:5–6 NLT

Do you consider yourself one of God's girls? If so, listen up! God's girls always tell the truth. Why? Because it's the right thing to do, even when it's the hard thing to do.

It's especially important to tell the truth when you're tempted to make up a little fib.

You might say, "Well, I don't lie! That's not a problem for me." Many of God's girls don't think they lie, but here's one way they slip up: they go around telling people they are Christians, but then they don't always act like it. Ouch! "So that's a lie?" you ask. Yep! Our words and our actions have to match up.

Imagine meeting a new girl at school. She tells you she's a Christian, and you're so excited to have a new friend. You sit next to each other in class and share all of your best secrets. You invite her to your house for a sleepover. Then you see her doing something really bad—maybe lying to the teacher or stealing something. You're confused by her actions. They don't match up with her words. She said she was a Christian. . .but she's not acting like one.

Christians must be people of truth who do what they say. We have to let the light of truth shine bright!

Lord, I want to shine bright. That means I have to tell the truth. . .always.
I need to do what I say I'm going to do. For that I need Your help, Father!

PLAYING FAVORITES

My friends, if you have faith in our glorious Lord Jesus Christ,
you won't treat some people better than others.
JAMES 2:1 CEV

. . . .

Do you play favorites? Maybe you have a special friend. You treat her nicer than you treat others. Sounds okay, right? Yet the Bible says that we are not to play favorites. That doesn't mean you shouldn't have a special friend. It just means that you have to treat others with the same kindness.

There's a story in the Bible about a man who comes into the church, wearing expensive clothes. He's treated better than the poor man because he's rich. God doesn't like this at all! We are to treat all people the same—no matter how they dress, how much money they have, or how many friends they have. We can't play favorites because we like how someone's skin and body look, either. God loves people in every color, shape, and size.

So don't play favorites. Don't treat some people good and other people bad. Love all people the same. God does, you know! And you want to be like Him, right? All right, then! No favorites!

. . . .

Lord, I have special friends, and I love them so much. Sometimes it's hard
to remember that You want me to love everyone equally as much.
Help me to do that, Lord. I want to love like You do!

DISCOURAGEMENT

I have told you this, so that you might have peace in your hearts because of me. While you are in the world, you will have to suffer. But cheer up! I have defeated the world.
JOHN 16:33 CEV

Have you ever been really discouraged? Maybe you just felt depressed. You couldn't seem to smile, no matter what. Even your goofy brother or silly sister couldn't get you to laugh. You just felt down in the dumps.

You are certainly not alone. We all go through seasons of discouragement. God understands what that feels like. Surely He gets a little sad when He sees His kids (us) wandering away from Him.

So how can you lift your spirits when you're down? What will it take to turn a sad day into a happy one? The answer is simple: praise the Lord. Might sound hard, but when you're really, really discouraged, instead of whining and complaining about how unhappy you are, instead of griping about your situation, begin to thank God that He has an answer. He does, you know. Trust Him. Praise Him. And He'll pick you up.

Father, sometimes I feel depressed. Other people around me are happy, but I'm not. I want to curl up in a ball and cry. During those discouraging times, please remind me that I can praise You, Lord! I will choose to praise. . .not complain.

JOY CHOOSERS

Therefore my heart is glad and my tongue rejoices;
my body also will rest secure.
PSALM 16:9 NIV

If you're like most girls, you have a lot of friends, and none of them are alike! Some are silly, some are sad. Some are happy, some are mad. Some are positive, others are negative. Those negative ones aren't much fun to be around, are they?

The best kind of friend is the one who chooses joy, no matter how tough things are. She always seems to walk above her circumstances with a smile on her face. She's not faking it. Not at all. Chances are she's really happy from the inside out because she has the joy of the Lord in her heart. She knows she can trust God, even when things are hard.

So here's an important question: Are you a joy chooser? Do people want to be around you because you lift their spirits by choosing joy, even when you're going through tough stuff? Why not ask God to fill you up with joy so that you can be known to your friends as a real joy chooser!

Lord, things in my life aren't perfect,
but that's okay. Today I choose joy anyway!

GOOD FRUIT, BAD FRUIT

*"Make a tree good and its fruit will be good, or make a tree bad
and its fruit will be bad, for a tree is recognized by its fruit."*
MATTHEW 12:33 NIV

. . . .

Did you ever take a bite of an apple and find out it was rotten on the inside?
Icky! There's nothing more disgusting than rotten old fruit. Ever eat a brown,
squishy banana? How about a dried-up orange, a mushy strawberry, or a moldy
peach? Gross, right?

So why are we talking about fruit? What does this have to do with
anything? Maybe more than you know! People recognize us by our fruit.
We're not talking about apples and oranges here. We're talking about the
fruits of the Spirit: love, joy, peace, patience, kindness, goodness, self-control,
faithfulness, and gentleness. If you stick close to Jesus (like vines clinging
to the branch of a tree), you will produce good fruit, but if you wander far
away, you will produce bad fruit.

Here's the thing: when people look at you, they either see someone who
shows love, joy, and patience, or they see someone who's grumpy, hard to get
along with, and impatient! They are seeing your fruit—good or bad! They see
either someone who has a helpful attitude or someone who always wants to
get her own way.

So which is it, sweet girl? Good fruit? Bad fruit? Happy fruit? Or sad
fruit? The decision is yours.

. . . .

Lord, please help me produce good fruit! When people look at me,
I want them to see love, joy, peace, patience, and all of
the other yummy things I should be producing!

WORTHY IS THE LAMB!

Then I looked and heard the voice of many angels, numbering thousands upon thousands, and ten thousand times ten thousand. They encircled the throne and the living creatures and the elders. In a loud voice they were saying: "Worthy is the Lamb, who was slain, to receive power and wealth and wisdom and strength and honor and glory and praise!"

REVELATION 5:11–12 NIV

Do you ever think about what heaven will be like? The Bible says there will be streets made of gold and a gate made of pearls! Gorgeous! One of the most amazing stories about heaven is found in the book of Revelation (in your Bible). In that story, a large group of angels and other worshippers are gathered around the throne of God, singing praises at the top of their lungs. Can you picture what that looks like?

Imagine the most amazing praise and worship service you've ever attended. Maybe it was at church, maybe at camp. Perhaps you closed your eyes as you sang worship songs to Jesus. Surely you felt His presence. Well, imagine that times a million or a billion! To worship Jesus in heaven, surrounded on every side by angels and all of the believers throughout time, what a joy that will be! Oooh, do you get goose bumps just thinking about it?

God is worthy of our worship, not just in heaven, but here on earth too. So the next time you're in church and the singers begin to worship Him, join in the song! You'll be rehearsing for heaven!

Lord, I can't wait to worship with the angels. The next time I'm in church, remind me that my worship is a rehearsal for that amazing day when I sing with the angel choir!

PEOPLE WHO SPARKLE AND SHINE

Therefore my heart is glad and my tongue rejoices;
my body also will rest secure.

PSALM 16:9 NIV

Have you ever met a girl who seemed to sparkle and shine? You could look at her smiling face and just know she was filled with God's joy. Her bright eyes always seemed to shimmer and shine with God's love for others. People like that are such a delight to be around because they're beautiful from the inside out. They're not pretending to be happy when they're not—they really, really are!

Here's some amazing news: you can *be* that girl! You can sparkle for Jesus. Just imagine your face being like a stained-glass window. When you're filled with God's joy from the inside out, you shimmer and shine for everyone to see. You look gorgeous because you're loaded with inner beauty, and it sparkles, sparkles, sparkles like the sun shining through a beautiful window. Talk about a heavenly glow! Why, everyone will want to know why you're shining like a star!

Father, I want to shimmer and shine for You! I want to be so filled
with joy that people see my bright eyes and big smile
and they say, "Wow! I want that joy too!"

A PINCH OF SALT

"You are the salt of the earth. But if the salt loses its saltiness, how can it be made salty again? It is no longer good for anything, except to be thrown out and trampled underfoot."

MATTHEW 5:13 NIV

Imagine you're at a fast-food place and have just ordered a cheeseburger and french fries. You taste the fries, only to discover there's no salt on them. In fact, you can't find salt anywhere in the restaurant. Sure, you go ahead and eat the fries, but they're not very tasty, are they? And it's not like you need a lot of salt to fix the problem. Just a little bit would go a long, long way.

Did you know that God wants you to be salty? It's true! When you're salty, you can share your faith with people who don't know the Lord and they will like the taste of what you're saying. Just a pinch here and there goes a long, long way. They don't need you to preach to them. (Talk about overloading the salt!) They just need little sprinkles, enough to make them thirsty for God. Problem is, some girls have lost their saltiness. They're so busy trying to fit in with their friends that no one notices they're any different at all.

God wants to use you to make people thirsty for Him. Sounds like fun, right? It is! What an adventure! So grab that saltshaker, kiddo! God's got work for you to do!

Father, I want to be a salty Christian! I want others to hear Your Good News and want what I have. Help me not to lose my flavor, Lord.

Too Much Stuff

Do not love the world or anything in the world.
If anyone loves the world, love for the Father is not in them.

1 JOHN 2:15 NIV

Girls sure have a lot of stuff! Their rooms are filled with it! But do you really need all of those things? Ever think about giving up some of your stuff?

Could you live without television? What about computers? The Internet? Cell phones? Video games? Could you manage without your cool shoes, your tablets, and your toys? What would you do if all of those things disappeared—never to return? Would your life be harder or easier?

Girls today have lots and lots of stuff, but some of it keeps them from doing what they should be doing. Imagine you're playing a video game. The hours go by and you don't even realize it. Before long, the whole afternoon has passed. You've missed out on spending time with your family or reading your Bible. You haven't done your homework, and you forgot to write that letter to your grandmother.

See how our "stuff" gets in our way? And here's the problem: we have trouble giving it up because we think we can't live without it. Now here's the fun challenge: for one full day, give something up! Don't think you can? Give it a try! After all, it's just stuff!

Father, I have to admit that I have a lot of stuff!
I don't really need all of it. Some of it steals my time.
Help me to love only You, Lord—not my stuff!

COMMITMENT

Commit your way to the Lord; trust in him, and he will act.
PSALM 37:5 ESV

Have you ever heard the word *commitment* before? Do you know what it means to be committed to something? When you're committed, it means you won't quit, no matter what! If you were committed to saving money for a mission trip, for instance, you would save, save, save instead of spend, spend, spend! If your mom is committed to losing weight, she doesn't give up, even when she's staring at a giant piece of chocolate cake! When your dad is committed to providing for his family, he gets out of bed every morning and goes to work, even when he doesn't feel like it.

Yes, to commit to something means you won't quit. So what does that mean for you, as a daughter of God? It means you will walk with Him and listen to His Word (the Bible) even when you don't feel like it. You will live a holy life, even when others around you are tempting you to do things you shouldn't. You will tell others about Him, even when it's hard.

Being committed is tough, but the rewards are great! So make up your mind! Don't quit! Decide today that you will stick close to God every day for the rest of your life! And He'll stick close to you—forever and ever!

Lord, I'm not a quitter. When I start something, I want to stick with it!
I started my relationship with You when I gave You my heart.
I commit to sticking with You forever, Father!

AN EXTRA DOSE

*So we have been greatly encouraged in the midst of our
troubles and suffering, dear brothers and sisters,
because you have remained strong in your faith.*

1 THESSALONIANS 3:7 NLT

. . . .

Do you ever feel like a weakling? Worn out and tired? Ready to give up? Do you sometimes need an extra dose of strength and courage? If so, join the club!

We all go through times when our faith is low, when we don't feel like we have the energy to pray for the big stuff. The tough stuff. But here's the cool thing about God: when we are at our very weakest, He is still strong. It's so cool to know that God never gets tired. He wants you to lean on Him when you're weak. And to trust Him to take over.

Let's say you have a big prayer need—a huge one. Maybe someone in your family is really sick or your parents are going through a crisis. Maybe you've prayed and prayed, but nothing seems to be happening. Even if you feel like your strength is gone, remember that God hasn't changed. He's still right there, on the throne, and He will strengthen you if you ask Him to. So ask! Approach the throne of your Daddy God and ask Him for courage to get you through the storms you are facing.

. . . .

God, sometimes I need an extra dose of faith. I feel like such a weakling.
Remind me that I'm strong in You, Father! Meanwhile I
will keep praying, keep believing, keep trusting.

TREASURE MAP

Oooh, buried treasure! Wouldn't you love to hunt for one? Sounds like a blast, right?

Imagine a map of a desert island, one that would lead you to the greatest buried treasure ever found. You follow the map until you come to a place where you dig for, then find, an old chest. It's filled with priceless gold coins and beautiful jewels worth millions of dollars. What would you do after cashing in all that treasure? Would you go shopping? Maybe you would spread the joy by taking your friends out for ice-cream sundaes! Or maybe you would help your parents pay the bills. What joy, to share your treasure with others!

The Bible says the kingdom of heaven is like a treasure hidden in a field. It is a thing of great value. When you come into a relationship with Jesus, you've discovered the greatest treasure of all—one that will lead you to heaven one day. The Christian life is a priceless gift, one you can't take for granted.

And guess what! God wants you to share that gift with others. So be sure to leave a clear trail for them to follow so that they too will one day discover this awesome treasure, one worth far more than millions of dollars!

Lord, thank You for giving me a treasure map (Your Word) so that I can go on this adventurous journey to discover eternal life. Help me leave a clear trail so that my friends can discover eternal life too!

LAYING DOWN YOUR LIFE

*This is how we know what love is: Jesus Christ laid down
his life for us. And we ought to lay down our lives
for our brothers and sisters.*

1 JOHN 3:16 NIV

When you hear the words *lay down your life,* what do you think of? Sounds kind of scary, doesn't it? But laying down your life for someone else just means that you put her first. You care more about her needs than your own.

Here's an example: Imagine your grandma is really sick. You are asked to go to her house to care for her. Let's be honest. . . you really don't want to do it. Sounds depressing. Maybe you'd rather hang out with your friends or play video games. But you go because you know you should.

When you arrive, you realize that your grandmother really needs a lot of help. She can't fix her own meals or mop her floors. She can't wash the dishes, and she even has trouble getting in and out of bed. When she sees that you've come to help her, she is so happy to see you, so very happy that she begins to cry!

Suddenly, looking into her eyes, you get it. You understand what it means to lay down your life for someone else. You will do whatever she needs—not just because it's the right thing to do, but because you love her.

Lord, I am learning how to put others' needs first.
Laying down my life isn't easy, but it's so worth it!

QUICK TO LISTEN

Understand this, my dear brothers and sisters: You must all be quick to listen, slow to speak, and slow to get angry. Human anger does not produce the righteousness God desires.

JAMES 1:19–20 NLT

Are you one of those girls who loves to be the center of attention? Do you like to be the one doing all of the talking, interrupting others when it's not really your turn? Well, listen up! The Bible says that God's daughters need to be quick to listen and slow to speak. That means you've got to be silent long enough to pay attention to what others are saying.

Time to be completely honest, girl, as you answer these questions: (1) Is it hard for you to be quiet when others are talking? (2) What happens when your feelings get hurt? Do you spout off like a teakettle boiling over? Do certain words come flying out of your mouth, ones you wish you could take back afterward?

It's hard to un-say something, isn't it? Better not to say it in the first place! So when you are hurt or angry, take a deep breath! Count to three! Don't speak without carefully thinking about what you're going to say. And remember that God's girls are quick to listen!

It's hard for me to admit this, Lord, but sometimes I like being the center of attention. Please help me to be slow to speak and quick to listen!

I'M STARVING!

The voice out of Heaven spoke to me again: "Go, take the book held open in the hand of the Angel astride sea and earth." I went up to the Angel and said, "Give me the little book." He said, "Take it, then eat it. It will taste sweet like honey."
REVELATION 10:9 MSG

What if you found out you couldn't eat all day? Not one bite of food. What would you do? Would you make it? What if you couldn't eat for two days...or three? Then what? Chances are, you would be mighty weak! You'd probably also be cranky. (Some people start to grumble after missing just one meal!) Before long, your hunger would take over and you wouldn't be able to think about anything—except food! (Can you hear your tummy growling?)

Did you know that the Bible (the Word of God) is like food to our spirits? Seriously. If you go without reading it for a while, you get weak. And if you go without reading it for a very long time, your strength is completely zapped. So don't let your Bible sit there on the bedside table gathering dust. Dive in, princess! A daughter of the King knows her Father's words. She memorizes them and quotes them when she needs a reminder that He's close by.

Feeling hungry? Reach for your Bible. Talk about a balanced diet!

I get so hungry sometimes, Lord! When I do, remind me that the yummiest thing I can munch on is Your Word. It will fill me up and lift my spirits, all at the same time!

SPEAK THE TRUTH!

Truthful lips endure forever,
but a lying tongue lasts only a moment.
PROVERBS 12:19 NIV

Do you promise to tell the whole truth and nothing but the truth, no matter what? Might sound impossible, but that's what God expects from His girls. You have to tell the whole truth, not just a half-truth! "Oh, but I don't tell lies!" you say. Maybe not, but sometimes actions speak louder than words!

Imagine this: Your best friend is sitting next to you in class and she looks over at your test, wanting to copy the answers. You're embarrassed and nervous, especially when the teacher notices and asks you what's going on. It would seem easier to tell a little white lie than confess the truth, wouldn't it—especially since you know your best friend will be mad at you for telling on her? Surely you can get away with a little lie just this once. Right?

Wrong! The problem with little white lies is there's nothing little about them! They're huge in God's sight. More important, He sees all the way down to the heart. That means God knows when we're being dishonest, even if no one else does—and it breaks His heart.

Dare to be different—especially in the tough times! Speak the truth!

Lord, I want to be a truth teller. Help me in the hard situations, Father. I want to tell the whole truth—and nothing but the truth!

CHRISTMAS STORY

*"There is born to you this day in the city of David
a Savior, who is Christ the Lord."*

LUKE 2:11 NKJV

Don't you just love the Christmas story? Mary, a simple young woman, is told by an angel that she's going to give birth to the Son of God. Joseph, the man she is engaged to marry, has to trust that the Lord knows what He's doing! Together, they make a journey to Bethlehem, riding on a donkey. When they arrive, Mary gives birth to baby Jesus—not in a hospital, not in a fancy hotel room, but in a lowly stable, next to the horses and cows! Wow, what a story!

Here's the coolest part: shepherds and wise men came to worship the new baby. Why would people worship a baby? Because they knew that this Child was different. . .special. Jesus was the Son of God!

So here's an interesting question: If the baby born in the manger was the Son of God, why just worship Him at Christmastime? Shouldn't we worship Him all year round? Yes! We should! And we do, every time we come together in church to sing praises! You can worship Him right where you are. Yes, you! Right now! Jesus is worthy of your praise, not just on December 25 but every day of your life!

Father, thank You for sending Your Son to this earth! Jesus lived
a perfect life! I'm so glad to know that I can worship Him,
not just at Christmastime but all year round!

ME? STUCK UP?

Nothing should be done because of pride or thinking about yourself.
Think of other people as more important than yourself.

PHILIPPIANS 2:3 NLV

As a daughter of the King, you are a real princess! That sounds great, right? Problem is, some girls take the whole "princess" thing a little too far. C'mon! You know it happens. Girls—even Christian girls—sometimes act a little, well, stuck up. They think they're "all that" (better than the others in their group). Maybe you've met girls like that. Maybe you've *been* a girl like that.

If you've struggled with being stuck up, it's time for a change! That's because the Bible teaches us to think of *others* as better than *ourselves*, the exact opposite of what a stuck-up girl thinks. It's hard, but true! If we're only focused on ourselves (our clothes, hair, popularity), we're not really thinking of others, are we? Nope. We're "stuck" on ourselves!

Today's verse shows us that we're not supposed to do anything out of conceit. That means we are not to brag about ourselves. We aren't to go around putting others down to make ourselves look better. (Oh, I know it's tempting!) We have to remember that God wants us to put others first. When we live like that, we're "stuck" on Him, not ourselves!

Father, I don't want to be "stuck" on myself. What matters most
is loving others. Help me to do that every single day, Lord!

DON'T WORRY, BE HAPPY!

"Therefore do not worry about tomorrow, for tomorrow will worry about itself. Each day has enough trouble of its own."

MATTHEW 6:34 NIV

Have you ever heard the expression "Don't be a worrywart"? If so, you probably get upset over things before they even happen. You fear the worst.

So are you a worrywart? Let's find out.

Imagine you've got a big math test coming up. Math isn't your best subject. You study, but you're still worried you won't do well. The night before the test, you can hardly sleep. You toss and turn for hours, fretting over how you will do on the test. What kind of grade you will make. What your teacher will say. How your parents will react. You start to imagine all sorts of things. "Will I pass math this year? Will I fail?"

You can worry all night long, but it won't make things any better. In fact, it usually makes things worse! God tells us in His Word that we aren't supposed to worry about tomorrow. So leave it up to God to handle the tough stuff. Do the best you can. . .then rest easy.

Lord, I don't like to worry! It's takes all of the fun out of life. But sometimes I feel like I can't help but fret. Today I give my worries to You, Lord. Thank You for taking them and giving me Your peace in return!

BEAUTY OR BRAINS?

Charm is deceptive, and beauty does not last;
but a woman who fears the LORD will be greatly praised.

PROVERBS 31:30 NLT

. . . .

If you could choose between being pretty and being smart, which one would you pick? Tough choice, right?

Here's the truth: every girl wants to be pretty. She wants to look in the mirror and see a beautiful face staring back at her. Problem is, we worry too much about what we look like. Someday we will grow older. Our faces will wrinkle. Our bodies will look different. Will that mean we're not pretty? Absolutely not! God created us in His image, and He thinks every woman is gorgeous, no matter what she looks like on the outside.

We need to start thinking more about how we look on the inside. Do we have pure hearts? Nice attitudes? Wonderful things to say about others? These are the things that make us beautiful. It takes more brains to be sweet than it does to be sour, after all. So use your brains. And remember, God always thinks you're beautiful, no matter what!

. . . .

Lord, please remind me that I need to be more concerned about how I look on the inside, not the outside. I'm always beautiful to You, Father. So help me use my brains to remember that my beauty isn't the most important thing!

A PARTY IN HEAVEN

*"Likewise, I say to you, there is joy in the presence
of the angels of God over one sinner who repents."*

LUKE 15:10 NKJV

Have you ever been to a really cool party? Maybe it was a princess-themed birthday party. Or maybe a pirate-themed party for your brother. Maybe you went to a fabulous anniversary party for your parents where a band played a special song that they danced to.

Parties are a blast, aren't they? There's nothing as fun as celebrating with friends and family. Did you know that the Bible says there are parties going on in heaven? It's true! The angels love to celebrate and throw a huge party every time someone here on earth accepts Jesus as her Savior.

Think about that. When you gave your heart to the Lord—when you accepted Jesus Christ as Lord and Savior of your life—the angels in heaven celebrated! They threw a party bigger than any you've ever been to! We won't know until we get to heaven what an angel party looks like, but there's no doubt about it—those angels sure know how to celebrate!

Dear Lord, I can't wait to go to an angel party! It's so cool to think that the angels celebrated when I gave my heart to You. What fun!

A BEGGAR NAMED LAZARUS

"There was a rich man who was dressed in purple and fine linen and lived in luxury every day. At his gate was laid a beggar named Lazarus, covered with sores and longing to eat what fell from the rich man's table."

LUKE 16:19–21 NIV

What an interesting story about Lazarus, the poor beggar man. Nothing worked out for him in his earthly life. He was poor and sick and so very hungry. Starving, in fact! Lazarus begged for crumbs from the rich man's table. Just a few scraps would have made him happy. The rich man seemed to have it all together. He had everything a man could want.

As the story continues, we learn that both of the men die. Lazarus goes to heaven. The rich man goes to Hades and is in agony. There's a huge chasm (think of a big, deep crack) between heaven and Hades. The rich man could see across the crack to where Lazarus was enjoying his life in heaven, and the rich man begged for just a drop of water to cool his tongue, but the chasm was too big for Lazarus to reach him.

Here's the point: some people seem to have everything in this life, but in the end, the only thing that will matter is if they had a relationship with Jesus. Without that, they won't be in heaven. So all of the riches in the world won't save any one of us.

Father, I'm glad I have the one thing that will get me to heaven. I have a relationship with Your Son, Jesus. I am thankful that I will spend eternity with You!

A PLEASANT ATTITUDE

In all the work you are doing, work the best you can.
Work as if you were doing it for the Lord, not for people.
COLOSSIANS 3:23 NCV

Is there anything sweeter than a happy, pleasant attitude? Every girl looks beautiful to others when her attitude is gracious and kind. When your attitude is lousy, meaning you're in a sour frame of mind, that sourness spills over onto others. The same thing happens when you have a great attitude. The people around you are cheered up—because of you! Wow, what power you have, cheering others up with your pleasant disposition!

Okay, so not every day is great. Some days we feel a little grumpy. We don't feel like giving our best. Maybe today is like that for you. If so, why not do an "attitude check." Before you go out the door, make sure your attitude will lift others up—not bring them down. And remember, everything you do is really for God, not people. Remember that, and it will help keep things in focus!

Lord, I don't always have the best attitude. I admit it. Sometimes I'm just plain grumpy. Remind me every day that my attitude matters, and also remind me that everything I do, I do for You.

LEARNING FROM PAST MISTAKES

*I focus on this one thing: Forgetting the past and looking forward to what lies
ahead, I press on to reach the end of the race and receive the heavenly
prize for which God, through Christ Jesus, is calling us.*

PHILIPPIANS 3:13–14 NLT

If you're like most girls, you've made a few mistakes in your life. Okay, maybe more than a few. Did you realize you can actually learn some lessons from your mistakes? It's true! Those lessons can help you move on and make you stronger than before. In fact, if you learn your lesson well, you can be confident that you won't make *that* mistake again!

Some people never learn their lesson. They can't let go of what happened yesterday. They hang on to the mistakes they've made. When people do this, it's as if their feet are stuck in quicksand. They can't move forward.

So how do you learn your lesson? Easy. Ask anyone you've harmed to forgive you. Next, ask God to forgive you. Then accept His forgiveness and move on. Don't look back. That's it. Don't live in the past. What happened yesterday is behind you. Don't worry about it anymore. Once you have asked for forgiveness and God has forgiven you, it's over. Done with. No quicksand for you! In fact, you are free to run the race as never before! So keep on pressing. Keep moving forward. You've learned your lesson, girl!

Father, thank You for teaching me that I can be forgiven.
I don't have to live in the past. My mistakes happened.
They're done with. I've been forgiven and am pressing on!

TO YOUR FACE. . .BEHIND YOUR BACK

Don't bad-mouth each other, friends.
It's God's Word, his Message, his Royal Rule,
that takes a beating in that kind of talk.

JAMES 4:11 MSG

Imagine this: You're hanging out with your best friend, Katie, when a new girl named Jenna walks by. Katie makes a comment about Jenna's hair or maybe her clothes. You know you shouldn't bad-mouth anyone, even someone you don't know, but what's the harm in talking about her behind her back? She'll never find out, right?

We must treat people with kindness, whether we are standing in front of them or in a completely different room. We have to watch the words that come out of our mouth. God tells us in the Bible that we are to treat others the way we want to be treated. (This is called the "Golden Rule" or, as in the verse above, the "Royal Rule.")

So how do you want to be treated? Better watch out! If you dish it out (gossiping, bad-mouthing, or cutting people down), you're telling God that that's the way *you* want to be treated. Ouch! When you think about it like that, it sure doesn't sound like much fun, does it?

Okay, Lord. . .I have to confess, I sometimes talk about people behind
their backs. I don't treat them the way I want to be treated.
Please forgive me and help me to guard my tongue.

A TEST OF FAITH

*My Christian brothers, you should be happy when you have all kinds of
tests. You know these prove your faith. It helps you not to give up.*

JAMES 1:2–3 NLV

How do you feel about tests in school? They're not much fun, are they? Some
of our life tests aren't much fun, either, but we can sure learn a lot from them.

Wondering what a *life test* is? Here's a simple way to look at it: Have you
ever been through a really rough time—a time when you just kept waiting for
something good to happen but wondered if it ever would? The Bible tells us
that those troubles we have are a test of our faith. They are life tests. They
teach us lessons. Sometimes we don't pass those tests! Yet we would be wise
if, while we're in the middle of them, we would be very patient. (To be patient
means to wait calmly for something to happen. You don't get all worked up
about it.) Waiting isn't always easy, especially if you're going through a life
test, but it is possible!

If you want to find out about someone who learned to be patient, read the
story of Job in the Old Testament. Talk about a guy who went through struggles!
He had lots of life tests. (Most of them were like pop quizzes—he never saw
them coming!) *And* he had to wait a long time for good things to happen.

Patience, girl! Learn from Job. . .and don't let those life tests get the best
of you!

Lord, I'm not crazy about taking tests, especially life tests. But I know some
tests are going to come. I just ask that You give me the patience
to get through them and the hope to see beyond them.

PRINCESS FOR A DAY

*"The Spirit Himself bears witness with our spirit
that we are children of God, and if children, then heirs—
heirs of God and joint heirs with Christ."*
ROMANS 8:16–17 NKJV

Have you ever wished you could be a princess for just a day? Have people wait on you hand and foot? Do whatever you liked? Eat whatever you wanted? Not have any worries in the world? Sounds like a blast, doesn't it?

Here's a little secret: you *are* a princess! You are a daughter of the One True God. You are His child! And He's the King of the universe, which would make you a royal princess—not just today but every day of the year.

So what does it mean to be a princess? Do you wear a ball gown and wave at your royal subjects? Do you expect people to wait on you and meet your every need? Nope! A daughter of the King knows that the greatest joy on earth is serving others. So instead of hoping people will wait on you, enjoy caring for others.

Lord, I have to admit, it sounds like a lot of fun to live in a castle and be
a princess. And that whole thing about being waited on. . .well, I guess
I can understand that it's even more fun to care for others.
Help me to have that servant's heart, Father!

R-E-S-P-E-C-T

*Dear brothers and sisters, honor those who are your leaders
in the Lord's work. They work hard among you
and give you spiritual guidance.*

1 THESSALONIANS 5:12 NLT

Have you ever thought about the word *respect*? Do you know what it means to respect your elders (those who are older than you)? Think about the adults you know. . .your parents, grandparents, and church leaders. Do you realize God has placed them in your life for a reason? And He's watching you closely to make sure you treat them with the respect they deserve.

Imagine this: A leader at your church (maybe your Sunday school teacher or kids' church pastor) isn't getting a lot of respect from the kids in the class. Maybe some of your friends are talking when they should be listening, or maybe they are interrupting when the teacher is speaking. What can you do to help? By far the best thing you can do is treat the teacher with respect. Then encourage others to do the same. Don't be part of the problem—be part of the solution. The teacher will be so grateful, and pretty soon many of the kids will follow your lead.

So why treat your leaders with respect? Because it's the right thing to do!

Lord, I pray that I will have a respectful heart.
May I always treat the adults in my life with
the kind of respect they deserve.

FESS UP!

If we confess our sins, he is faithful and just to forgive us our sins.

1 JOHN 1:9 ESV

Have you ever heard someone say, "Confession is good for the soul"? Maybe you've heard it but don't know what it means. To confess something means you admit it to someone. You say it out loud in front of another person. In other words, you tell what you've done—even if it's really, really hard to do so.

Need an example? Imagine you've done something bad. Really bad. Maybe you snuck into your mom's room and "borrowed" her favorite earrings then lost them. You haven't told anyone about it. . .you wouldn't dare. If people knew, it would change the way they think about you. And besides, some secrets are okay to keep, right? That's what you tell yourself, anyway!

Only, you're wrong. It's not good to keep this kind of secret. According to today's Bible verse, it's better to get it off your chest. Tell someone who loves you. And don't give them the watered-down version, either. Tell her the whole ugly story, even the parts that are hardest to share. She might be shocked, but that's okay. God will help you as you make your confession. Afterward, ask her to pray that you will be stronger the next time you're tempted.

There, now! Doesn't that feel better? Feel that weight lifted? Confessing your sins is good for your health! And your family and friends will respect you for being so open and honest.

Oh Lord, it's so hard to confess the bad things I've done! I'd rather keep them to myself, but I know that You can help me when I open up and share. I need Your help and Your courage, Father!

LOST SHEEP

"What do you think? If a man owns a hundred sheep, and one of them wanders away, will he not leave the ninety-nine on the hills and go to look for the one that wandered off?"
MATTHEW 18:12 NIV

There's a cool story in the New Testament about a shepherd who has one hundred sheep. He loves watching all of them, but let's be honest—sheep are hard to control! They want to do their own thing!

In the story, ninety-nine of the sheep stick together, but one little sheep wanders away from the others and gets lost. Man! If you were the shepherd, what would you do? Leave the ninety-nine and go after the lost one, or let the little lost sheep try to find his way back alone? After all, if you leave the ninety-nine, one of them might wander off.

If you keep reading the story, you see that the shepherd leaves the ninety-nine sheep and goes to search for the missing one. Wow! Did you realize that story is about more than just sheep? God is trying to tell us He loves us so much that if we wander away from Him, He will come and look for us to protect us. So the next time you are tempted to do something you know you shouldn't, remember. . .God wants you to stick with the other sheep (other Christians), not wander off into sin. Don't make Him come looking for you! Stay close to His side, and let the Shepherd care for you.

Father, please forgive me for the times I wander off. Sometimes I'm tempted to do things I shouldn't. Help me to remember the story of the sheep and the shepherd. I want to stay close by You, Lord!

CHORES

All hard work brings a profit,
but mere talk leads only to poverty.
PROVERBS 14:23 NIV

There's something about the word *chores* that sends a shiver down your spine. When you hear the word *chores*, you probably think of work, work, work. But think about how much work you would have to do if you didn't do your chores.

Here's an example: Let's say you didn't pick up your clothes off the floor for a couple of days. Okay, make that five days. Maybe even six days. After a while, you would run out of clean clothes. There would be nothing to wear. A girl can only wear the same dirty clothes so many days in a row before they get stinky! Gross, right?

But if you pick up the dirty clothes and put them in the laundry basket, they can get washed. Sure, it's a chore to take care of this every day, but it's so worth it! After all, it's better than running out of clean clothes and having to wear old stinky ones!

Is it starting to make sense now? Chores keep us disciplined, and they also keep the mess from stacking up and getting smelly!

Lord, I really don't like to do my chores. Making my bed is no fun.
Neither is picking up toys and clothes and shoes. But I'm learning that
chores are really good for me, Father. Help me to remember that daily!

MONEY

The love of money causes all kinds of trouble. Some people want money so much that they have given up their faith and caused themselves a lot of pain.
1 TIMOTHY 6:10 CEV

Have you ever heard people say that money is evil? Money, itself, isn't evil at all. In fact, we can use money to feed the poor, put clothes on children who need them, buy shoes for people who have none. We can use money to travel to other countries to tell people about Jesus.

No, money isn't bad. But the *love* of money is.

So what does it mean to love money? Does it mean you carry dollar bills in your pocket and pull them out, covering them in kisses? Not at all! "Love of money" means you care about the things that money can buy more than you should. For instance, you love designer clothes so much that you think about them day and night. You love a certain pair of shoes so much that you want them more than you want to take care of the needs of others.

Having money is one thing. Loving it is another. So if you're struggling with loving it too much (c'mon, we all go through it!), you need to ask God to forgive you. He can change your focus—from loving stuff to loving people and caring enough to put their needs above your own.

Dear Lord, I have to confess I love having money to spend on myself.
I like buying myself special presents. If I ever start loving the
things money can buy too much, Father, please stop me!

A Lovely Gift

A wise son brings joy to his father,
but a foolish man despises his mother.

PROVERBS 15:20 NIV

Have you ever had trouble trying to figure out the perfect gift for someone you love? Are you looking for something you can give your mom or dad this Christmas? Something sure to make them hap–hap–happy? Try wisdom. It's the perfect gift!

No, you don't need to give *them* wisdom. You need to get it for yourself. The wiser you are, the happier your parents will be. They will be thrilled to see you wising up!

So what does it mean to act wisely? It means making excellent choices! Treating your brothers and sisters the way you want to be treated. Even though it may be hard, it means not insisting on having things your own way. It's doing the things you're told (without having to be told twice). It also means offering to help out when your parents are tired. These are all things that prove you're very, very wise.

Are you wondering where wisdom comes from? Why, from your heavenly Father, of course! All you have to do is ask, and He will give you wisdom. Read His Word (the Bible). It's loaded with nuggets of wisdom. Then pray. Ask His opinion about absolutely everything. This is by far the wisest thing you can do.

Father, thank You for showing me how to be wise. I want to share
the gift of wisdom and make my parents very, very happy!

Tossing the Masks

*"Nothing is covered up that will not be revealed,
or hidden that will not be known."*

LUKE 12:2 ESV

Have you ever pretended to be someone you're not? Maybe you find yourself acting like others instead of just being yourself. This is called "putting on a mask." Oh, it's not a real mask, like one you would wear to a party. It's an invisible one. No one knows you're wearing it except you!

So why do we put on masks, anyway? Why is it so hard just to be ourselves? Sometimes we do so to cover up pain. We pretend to be happy when we're really not. Sometimes we do it to be accepted. We act like our friends so they will like us. Truth is, there's never a good reason to put on a mask. God wants you... to be you. No one else.

Sometimes the best mask you can wear is your own face with real, honest emotions. No covering up. No pretending. Just honesty.

I get tired of pretending to be something I'm not, Lord. Help me accept that it's okay to just be me. No more masks, Father! I toss them all in the trash.

LEMONADE MAKERS

For everything that was written in the past was written to teach us,
so that through the endurance taught in the Scriptures and
the encouragement they provide we might have hope.
ROMANS 15:4 NIV

Have you ever heard the old expression about turning lemons into lemonade? Whenever life gives you something sour (when things don't go your way), you can either cry. . .or turn the sour lemons into lemonade (something sweet).

How do you turn sour things sweet? Easy! It's all about the attitude, girl! Change your attitude to a sweet one and watch the situation, even one that's really, really sour, turn around.

Some people don't do a very good job of handling bad days. They give in to the pressures and become grumpy sourpusses. But not you! Nope! You can turn lemons into lemonade. In fact, you've learned to love lemonade!

Lord, thank You for showing me how to change my sometimes lousy
attitude. I don't want to be an old picklepuss, Father. Help me
turn sour days around by adding a spoonful of sugar!

LISTEN UP, KIDDO!

Listen, my son, to your father's instruction and do not forsake your mother's teaching. They are a garland to grace your head and a chain to adorn your neck.

PROVERBS 1:8–9 NIV

Has this ever happened? You're focused on a television show or a video game and your mom is trying to talk to you. You hear her. Sort of. But you're really not paying attention. Why? Because your mind is on other things. You're distracted.

To really listen means you really pay attention to what's being said to you. You're not planning your next slumber party or thinking about who you're going to the mall with. You're not playing a video game or sending a text message to someone. When you're really listening, you hear everything the other person says. Every single word. You are giving her your full, undivided attention, and you're doing it because what she's talking about is important to you. You care.

You have so much to learn from the adults in your life. When your parents ask for your attention, it's often because they're trying to teach you something. The best way you can show them you're learning is to do what they say. In other words, to listen means to obey. So listen up!

Lord, I confess I don't always listen to what other people are saying. I'm busy thinking about other things. Please help me to listen up, Father!

STAYING STRONG

So Delilah said to Samson, "Tell me the secret of your great
strength and how you can be tied up and subdued."
JUDGES 16:6 NIV

Have you ever read the Bible story about a really strong man named Samson? Because he had taken a vow never to cut his hair, it was super long. Not only that, Samson knew that cutting off his hair would take his strength away. (Interesting, right?)

Samson's enemies knew about his muscle but didn't know its source. Wanting to defeat him, they sent a wicked woman named Delilah to tempt Samson, pretending to be in love with him. She kept nagging him, wanting him to tell her what made him so strong. Finally he told her his secret. Later, she waited until he was sleeping and then cut off his hair. Man! Some friend she was! When he woke up, the hairless and now weak Samson was captured by his enemies.

What does this have to do with us? Are we supposed to keep our hair long so that we will be strong? Not exactly. Here's the point: God has told us to be on the watch for people who want to make us weak. We shouldn't be hanging around people who could bring us down or make us frail in our faith. Instead, we need to remain strong.

In the end, Samson won his battle. He got his strength back and defeated his enemies. But what a lesson he had to learn along the way.

Lord, I don't want to give in to temptation. I want to remain strong in You. Please remind me not to hang around with people who will bring me down.

PURE LAUGHTER

"He will yet fill your mouth with laughter,
and your lips with shouting."

JOB 8:21 ESV

There are so many gifts you can share with others, but probably one of the best is laughter. Oh, you didn't know you could share laughter? You can! When you laugh with a friend or family member, you are sharing something much deeper than a good joke or a funny reaction to a situation. . .you're sharing a special bond. Laughter—good medicine for your heart, mind, spirit, and soul—connects you and others in a very deep and positive way. Your laughter bubbles up, up, up and, once out, is contagious! Before long everyone around you is laughing!

Here's something very important to remember: it's fun to laugh *with* someone, but it's never okay to laugh *at* someone. Poking fun at someone is mean-spirited, and it's not something God likes. So just make sure your laughter comes from a pure heart. When God hears your giggles, it makes Him so happy!

Lord, I love to laugh. It's even more fun when I'm laughing with a friend.
Please help me remember that it's great to laugh with people,
but I should never laugh at them.

FOR YOUR OWN GOOD

The LORD disciplines those he loves,
as a father the son he delights in.

PROVERBS 3:12 NIV

"I'm doing this for your own good." How many times have you heard those words from parents, grandparents, or teachers? They usually precede them with other words you don't like to hear: "No, you can't spend the night with your friend," or "You have to clean up that messy room!" And almost every single time they add: "I'm doing this for your own good."

Whenever you hear these words, you know that your parents are disciplining you. In other words, they are taking the time to correct your behavior. Maybe you were supposed to clean up your room days ago, but didn't. Now it's time to pay the piper. You can't spend the night with your best friend, and you've got to stay in your room all day, doing what you neglected earlier. Or maybe you were rude (or mean) to your little brother, and now you have to do extra chores (fold the clothes or wash the dishes).

If your parents didn't love you, they wouldn't discipline you. That's probably hard to understand, but it's true! If they didn't give you boundaries, you wouldn't know the difference between right and wrong. And, believe it or not, when your parents say, "I'm doing this for your own good!" they really are!

Lord, I don't always believe that discipline is for my own good. I need Your help in the moment to know that what's happening to me is really Your very best for my life.

CLEAN UP THAT MESS!

*You call out to God for help and he helps—he's a good Father that way.
But don't forget, he's also a responsible Father, and won't let
you get by with sloppy living.*

1 PETER 1:17 MSG

If you're a typical girl, you probably get tired of hearing the words "Clean up that mess!" Right? Most of us don't like to be told we're messy. And who cares, anyway? Why does it matter if you leave your wrinkled T-shirts wadded up in the corner or forget to make your bed? Then again, maybe your mom or dad is cool with that.

Well, listen up! It's one thing to leave your clothes on the floor. It's another thing to be sloppy in your spiritual life—forgetting to pray or skipping your Bible reading time. Sometimes we just get busy and forget. Right?

You are a daughter of the King, and your heavenly Father (just like your earthly parents) wants you to learn to be responsible. That means sloppy living—be it physical or spiritual—isn't cool. Clean up your act, princess! The next time you trip over a pair of dirty socks on the floor, use it as a reminder to pray. And the next time you look at that messy room, remember that God took the time to clean up your mess—your sin—when He sent Jesus, His Son, to die on the cross.

God, I don't want to be messy, in my physical or in my spiritual life.
If there are messes that need to be cleaned up, Lord,
show me, and then help me fix them.

103

DEFEATING ENEMIES

Keep your life free from love of money, and be
content with what you have, for he has said,
"I will never leave you nor forsake you."
HEBREWS 13:5 ESV

Have you ever read the story in the Bible about a man named Gideon? His name means "Destroyer" or "Mighty Warrior." God asked Gideon to do something hard—to tell the people that they needed to stop worshipping idols. (An *idol* is anything you treat as more important than God.) Gideon was very brave and did what God said. . .and he won the battle against evil.

What does this have to do with us? God wants up to stand up to the "idols" in our world too. "What sort of idols?" you may ask. Anything that people worship and adore could be an idol: clothes, money, popularity, shoes, talent—anything like that. Whenever we long for something more than we long for God, we're "idolizing" it.

So what do you do if you're surrounded by people who care more about their possessions than they do about God? Do you speak up like Gideon did, or do you remain silent? Maybe God is calling you to be a "Mighty Warrior" when you're around your friends. Don't go along with the crowd, longing for the "stuff" they want or already have. Instead, worship the One True God and watch Him make you victorious in the end!

Father, I want to be like Gideon, but it means I'll have to be brave.
I don't want to go along with the crowd or to "idolize" things.
The only One I want to worship is You, Lord!

THE WALLS CAME TUMBLING DOWN!

By faith the walls of Jericho fell, after the army
had marched around them for seven days.
HEBREWS 11:30 NIV

Have you ever faced a huge obstacle—one so big you couldn't see around it? You couldn't climb over it? Maybe you've got a learning disability. No matter how hard you work, you still struggle to make good grades. Or maybe you can't seem to handle science class. Or the numbers in math just won't add up. Don't get discouraged. Choose to believe that God is bigger than any*thing* you will ever face. Don't place any limitations on Him—or you!

There's a really cool story in the Bible about some huge walls surrounding a town called Jericho. The people of God marched around those walls for seven days, and guess what happened! The walls fell down!

What if we prayed for the walls to come falling down in our lives? If we looked beyond our limitations and saw ourselves the way God sees us? If we refused to give up when things go wrong? If we prayed in faith?

The next time you're going through a really hard time, remember that God is a God of the impossible! In fact, the Bible says He *delights* in doing the impossible! So even if you're facing a huge obstacle, choose to believe, and then watch those walls come tumbling down!

God, there are some pretty big walls in my life! And I need them to come
tumbling down. Give me the faith to speak to those walls so
that they can crumble to the ground!

MY SECRET PLACE

But Jesus often withdrew to lonely places and prayed.

LUKE 5:16 NIV

Imagine you're at a really fun back-to-school party and there are lots of people there. You see an old friend, someone you hardly ever get to talk to. She's been away all summer and you have a lot of catching up to do, so you go outside, away from the noise and confusion, so that you can spend some time together. Isn't it wonderful to visit—just the two of you? Alone together, you swap stories about the fun summer you had. What joy!

It's the same in your relationship with God. He longs to spend time with you. Whether you're with your friends, your family, or the people from your church, life can get really loud and crazy! Even though it's exciting to hang out with lots of people and have a great time, it's also wonderful to sneak away to that secret place for some quiet time with your heavenly Father. Alone together, He doesn't just want you to talk to Him; He wants you to listen. It's easier to hear His voice when you're quiet and still, which is why it's important to get away from the crowd.

By going to that secret place, you're letting God know that you, His princess, adore Him and really love hanging out with just Him. So break away from the crowd today—and do just that!

I love spending quiet time with You, Lord, away from the crowd.
I have a lot to tell You, and You have a lot to tell me too!

SOMEONE TO LISTEN

My son, listen to my words. Turn your ear to my sayings.
PROVERBS 4:20 NLV

Sometimes we just need a friend or loved one to sit with us while we're pouring our heart out. Doesn't it feel good to have someone listen, really listen? The problem is, others are usually so busy talking that they don't stop to really hear what we are saying to them. As we're talking, they're already thinking of what they're going to say.

Stop for a minute and think about your friends and family members. Who are the best listeners in the group? Who are the people who don't interrupt, who really care about what you're going through? Those are the people you can trust when you need someone to talk to. Don't be afraid to tap one of them on the shoulder and say, "Hey, do you have a few minutes? I need someone to listen."

Finding a good listener is great, but being a good listener is even better. The next time a friend needs you to listen, be prepared to do just that. . .listen.

Dear Lord, thank You for my friends who are willing to listen when I need to talk. And thank You for teaching me how to listen when they need me!

ENTERTAIN ME!

I will be careful to live an innocent life. When will you come to me?
I will live an innocent life in my house. I will not look at anything wicked.
PSALM 101:2–3 NCV

Having fun with friends is a blast, of course, but some girls take it w-a-y too far. All they want to do is play. Doing their homework, cleaning house, making their bed, spending time with family. . .none of that seems like much fun to them. Going to the movies, listening to music, watching TV shows, playing video games, spending countless hours on the Internet. . .these are the things they love!

Oh, and swim parties, slumber parties, bowling, roller skating. . .what a blast! You name it, these girls love, love, love to be entertained around the clock. Life is a party, after all! Right? No time for the serious stuff.

So what's wrong with being entertained all of the time? It's not a healthy way to live! When you waste so many hours doing things that don't really matter, you give away precious time that could be used in a better way. It's not wrong to relax and have fun, but if you're spending hours and hours doing so, you might want to reconsider.

Father, I'll admit it. . .I like to be entertained. Games and TV shows are fun. Going to the movies is fun too. Please help me to remember that there are much more important things I need to be doing with my time, Lord!

Do It Anyway

I can do all things through Christ who strengthens me.
PHILIPPIANS 4:13 NKJV

There are going to be lots of times when you will be asked to do something that you think you can't do. Maybe you're supposed to run a race but aren't sure you can make it to the finish line. So you hang up your sneakers. Or maybe you're supposed to write a report for school, but every time you look at the white piece of paper, your mind goes blank. You're convinced you can't do it, so why even try?

Here's a fun idea: do it anyway! Seriously. Instead of saying, "I can't!" practice saying, "I'm going to try anyway, no matter how things turn out!" Who knows! You might just be the fastest runner in town. Maybe you will end up being a writer when you grow up. You never know!

Think about all of the people who've done amazing things for God. The missionaries. The pastors. The singers. What if each of them had said, "I can't do it!" Thank goodness they didn't give up. So don't you give up, either. Remember, you can do all things through Christ. *He's* the One who gives you the strength. So what are you waiting for, girl? You've got this!

Lord, thank You for reminding me that I can do all things through Christ.
Please strengthen me and give me a do-it-anyway attitude.

GLAMOUR

But the Lord said to Samuel, "Do not look at the way he looks on the outside or how tall he is, because I have not chosen him. For the Lord does not look at the things man looks at. A man looks at the outside of a person, but the Lord looks at the heart."

1 SAMUEL 16:7 NLV

When you think of the word *glamour*, what comes to mind? Fashion models? Movie stars? A girl's fantastic makeup job? The latest fashions from Paris? The word *glamorous* refers to people who are exciting and beautiful to look at. They own expensive things. It can be fun looking at magazines that are filled with pictures of glamorous people and to daydream about what it would be like to be one of them. But in the real world, we need to watch out! Looking good on the outside isn't what matters to God!

So many want to spend time with the "pretty people." Let's face it. Girls want to hang out with other girls who are popular and cute, right? On the surface that might not be a big deal, but if you dig deeper, you see that God doesn't judge women—or men—that way. He doesn't care what we look like on the outside. He's interested in the inside—a pretty heart.

Do you want to be truly attractive to others, to have a pretty heart? There's one simple way to do this: love others. Love them, no matter what they look like. Love them unconditionally. (That means you love them whether they're good or bad, right or wrong.) Unconditional love is very glamorous.

Father, I want to learn to love people unconditionally! Help me not to judge others based on how they look.

110

A GREAT BOOK

*On the seventh day God ended His work which He had done. And He rested
on the seventh day from all His work which He had done. Then God
honored the seventh day and made it holy, because in it
He rested from all His work which He had done.*

GENESIS 2:2–3 NLV

Don't you love those cozy days when you have the time to settle in with a good book? There's something pretty awesome about being whisked away by a good story, isn't there? A good book is more than an escape. It's a place to dream, to hope, and to see new possibilities.

If you're looking for the very best book to read, here's a suggestion: the Bible! It's absolutely loaded with stories of people who did amazing things: Walking on water. Feeding five thousand people with five loaves of bread and two fish. Healing the sick. Raising the dead. All of this and much, much more. Wow! And the coolest part of all? These stories are true! They're not made up. They really happened to ordinary men and women who followed Jesus and learned from Him.

Aren't you glad that God spoke to the hearts of His people and they wrote down these cool stories so that we could read them? Maybe one day the Lord will speak to your heart to write down the miracles that take place in your life too. Then you can pass those stories on to your children, and their children, and their children's children!

Dear Lord, I'm so happy that I can read my Bible and discover true stories
of miracles. I'm also excited that You still perform miracles today!
I want to write them down so that I never forget!

DO-DO-DOER

I find rest in God; only he can save me. He is my rock and my salvation.
He is my defender; I will not be defeated.

PSALM 62:1–2 NCV

Have you ever met someone who loved to work? She would go-go-go around the clock if she could, working and accomplishing a lot! Maybe you're a do-do-doer. You work hard at everything! School. Sports. Family activities. Crafts. Do-do-doers are busy-busy-busy!

There's only one problem with do-do-doing so much. You don't have much time left over to rest or to pray. Maybe you think you don't need much rest. Maybe you think that a quick prayer here or there is enough. The truth is, you need both! Resting is so important to God that He actually created a whole day (the Sabbath) for it. But resting is about more than just kicking your feet up and taking time off from your work. It's about trusting God. It's about believing that He can save you. When you truly "rest" in Him, you can say, "I know You've got this, Lord!" and mean it!

The next time you feel like go-go-going, ask the Lord to show you when enough is enough. He might just speak to your heart and say, "Slow down, girl! There's plenty of time to do-do-do later. Right now, I just want you to spend time with Me."

Father, thank You for reminding me that it's a good thing to rest—
my body, my heart, and my mind. I know I can trust You,
and that brings me such peace.

A GOOD NIGHT'S SLEEP

If you lie down, you will not be afraid;
when you lie down, your sleep will be sweet.

PROVERBS 3:24 ESV

Most girls love curling up under the covers after a long day. Ahh, bliss! Is there anything more wonderful than getting a good night's sleep? How wonderful to snooze, snooze, snooze all night long with no interruptions. Nothing but eight blissful hours of *zzz*'s! Talk about an awesome way to rest after a hard day at school.

Did you know that the Bible is filled with scriptures about resting? It's true. God says that He wants your sleep to be sweet. Doesn't that sound amazing? *Sweet sleep* means you don't go to bed worried about anything. You're also not going to bed mad at anyone or feeling upset about anything. You're happy and content.

Maybe you have a lot on your mind today. You're afraid of something, or maybe you're mad at your brother or sister. Let go of that fear. Be quick to forgive! Give everything over to God so that tonight, when you settle into bed, you can have the best night's sleep ever!

God, I needed to be reminded that my sleep can be sweet! I want to rest
my head on the pillow tonight, not upset or fearful about anything.
Thank You for taking away my worries so that I can rest!

IT'S ALL ABOUT THE SEASONS

*There is a time for everything, and
a season for every activity under the heavens.*
ECCLESIASTES 3:1 NIV

. . . .

The Bible tells us that everything has its season. Maybe you've been waiting for something to happen, but it's just not the right season yet. You get frustrated because you want it to happen now. It feels like it's taking too long. Well, hang on, girl! Your day is coming!

Imagine you're in a springtime season. Everything in your life is blooming. You've got fun new friendships with the girls at your school, and you're growing in the Lord. Then summer comes. Everything is now sunny and in full bloom. You're in a great relationship with your parents and getting along well with your kid brother or sister.

Next comes fall. Maybe you notice that you're not as close to your best friend as you used to be, or maybe other things in your life are changing. Maybe you used to take ballet lessons and now you don't; or maybe you were in a choir and now you're not. After fall comes winter. If you're in a winter season, maybe nothing seems to be working out. Perhaps you're lonely or disconnected—having a hard time with your prayer life.

No matter what season you're in, remember. . .you can trust God to see you through.

. . . .

Father, thank You for reminding me that seasons don't last forever.
When I'm in a hard season, remind me that springtime is coming!

I'M PRAYING FOR YOU

I always thank my God as I remember you in my prayers.
PHILEMON 1:4 NIV

Have you ever been through a really hard time? Maybe you struggled with your math homework or had trouble in science class. Truth is, it's no fun going through tough times alone! Knowing that someone is praying for you really helps. There's such power in prayer!

What if you told your best friend (or maybe one of your parents) what you were going through in school and asked him or her to pray for you? Wouldn't that make you feel better? It always lifts your spirits to know someone else is lifting up your name in prayer. It also gives you courage and confidence to believe you're going to make it!

It works the other way around too. If you tell someone you're going to be praying for her, she's counting on you to really do it. So how do you know who to pray for? Try this: Put together a list. Don't forget to add your family members and friends from school and church. Don't stop there! Maybe there's an elderly neighbor in need of prayer. Now comes the fun part. Every day (at least once a day), sit down with your list and pray over every name. That's right! Lift up every name! There, doesn't that feel great?

Lord, thank You for the gift of prayer and for people who pray for me.
Help me to make a list of people I need to be praying
for. I don't want to leave anyone out!

THE GiRLy GiRL

"I will be your father, and you will be my sons
and daughters, says the Lord Almighty."
2 Corinthians 6:18 ncv

Some of us are just born girly girls. We're into hair, makeup, shoes, and all of the other frills that come along with the territory. Might seem a little silly to others, but getting all dressed up can be a lot of fun.

Did you ever wonder why girls love all the ribbons and bows? We're daughters of a King, you see! It's true! God, our Father, is King over all the earth. So that would make us princesses, and everyone knows that a princess loves her frills!

The best part of being a girly girl? Having compassion and kindness toward those who are not! Not everyone loves all of the frilly stuff. So whether you do or you don't, just remember that a princess (a daughter of the One True King) is gorgeous to her Father (God) whether she's all dressed up or wearing rags. He doesn't look down from heaven and say, "Hey, you! Why don't you put on a girly-girl dress and wear ribbons in your hair?" Nope. He's too busy saying, "Hey, daughter! I love you! You're beautiful to me!" Now that's a Dad a girl can love!

Oh Father, I'm so glad that You love me whether I'm a girly girl or not!
Help me to remember that I'm always beautiful to You!

MAKEUP. . .NOT THE KIND IN A BAG

They will rebuild the old ruins and restore the places
destroyed long ago. They will repair the ruined cities
that were destroyed for so long.

ISAIAH 61:4 NCV

Have you ever been through a breakup in a friendship? Maybe there's a certain girl you haven't spoken to in ages. You used to be good friends, but now you're not. Maybe you had a fight. Now you want to make up with her so that you can be friends again. Is it possible? You hope so, but you're not sure.

God loves it when His daughters get along! He thinks it's amazing when you forgive one another and become friends again. Don't think you can do it? Think it's too big for God? Remember, nothing's too big for Him, so pray and believe. Then reach into your "makeup" bag. Every girl has one, you know! It's called your heart! That's where you go to forgive and to make things right.

Take a look at today's scripture. You might wonder what old, ruined cities have to do with friendships. Maybe more than you know! God loves it when "old" things are rebuilt—whether it's cities, friendships, or lives. He's in the "rebuilding" business. So trust Him to put the pieces back together in your friendship. He's big enough to handle it!

Dear Lord, it's not always easy to make up with a friend after an argument.
But I know You're in the "rebuilding" business, so I'm trusting
You to restore my friendship. Nothing is too big for You!

STICK WITH GOD'S PEOPLE

*But Ruth said, "Do not urge me to leave you or to return from following
you. For where you go I will go, and where you lodge I will lodge.
Your people shall be my people, and your God my God."*

RUTH 1:16 ESV

Have you ever wondered why people spend so much time in church? They go on Sundays, sometimes twice! They go on Wednesday evenings. Some people even go on Saturdays or other days of the week. Does that seem like a lot of time to spend in church? It's not!

God loves it when His people hang out together. It makes His heart happy to see us singing worship songs, learning Bible lessons, and visiting. He knows that being together makes us unified. To be unified means we have a lot in common. We love the same things and enjoy being one big happy family. What a blast!

Take a look at today's scripture. A young woman named Ruth said these words to her mother-in-law, Naomi: "Where you go I will go, and where you lodge [live] I will lodge [live]. Your people shall be my people, and your God my God." When we go to church with other Christians, we are pretty much telling them the same thing: "I want to be with you. Your people are my people, and we serve the same awesome God!"

Father, I'm so happy You put me in such a great church. These are Your people! We're one big happy family. How awesome to serve You together!

MENDING FENCES

"If your brother sins against you, go and tell him his fault, between you and him alone. If he listens to you, you have gained your brother."
MATTHEW 18:15 ESV

Have you ever watched someone mend a broken fence? Maybe some pieces of wood were missing and had to be replaced, so he took a hammer and some nails and started working, working, working to make the fence perfect again.

Sometimes mending broken relationships is like fixing a broken fence. It takes work. Imagine this: Your friend did something that really hurt your feelings. Maybe she told a lie about you, and she won't admit it. What do you do?

The Bible teaches us that when we've been hurt by someone else, we need to go to that person—not to others, but to the very person who hurt us—and talk about it. You don't gossip to your other friends or make a big deal about it. Just go to the girl who in some way hurt you and say, "Hey, can we talk?" If she listens to you, then you may have won your friend back! But if you go to your other friends and start a bunch of gossip or in some other way pay back the one who harmed you, everything will just get worse. So have courage! Go to the one who has hurt your feelings and have a heart-to-heart chat. Then watch God mend those fences!

Father, thanks for reminding me to talk to the person who hurt me, not talk about her! Help me to choose that better way, Lord!

GREAT GIFTS

*"Which of you, if your son asks for bread, will give him a stone?
. . . .If you, then, though you are evil, know how to give good gifts
to your children, how much more will your Father in
heaven give good gifts to those who ask him!"*

MATTHEW 7:9, 11 NIV

Imagine Christmas is coming. You see all of the presents under the tree and are especially curious about the one wrapped in the pretty gold paper with your name on it. What in the world is inside? Oooh, it could be a new camera or some great new jeans. Maybe it's a computer or a video game. The suspense is too much to take! You can hardly wait for Christmas!

Finally the big day arrives. You are so excited! One by one the presents are opened until it's finally your turn. You reach for the package and tear away the paper, only to discover a dirty old tennis ball, chewed up by the dog. What? Confused, and a little hurt, you look at your parents. What kind of mom and dad would give their daughter a gift like that? Seriously?

Maybe this is a goofy example, but here's the point: Your parents would never give you a stinky old chewed-up tennis ball! They give you good gifts because they love you! And here's the cool part—God gives even better gifts if you ask! That's what the Bible says. Why? Because He loves you! So ask! You might be surprised at what God has in store for you!

Daddy God. . .You give great gifts! Even better than those on Christmas morning. I can hardly wait to see what wonders You have in store for me!

A TiGHT FiST

Give all your worries and cares to God,
for he cares about you.
1 PETER 5:7 NLT

Imagine you're holding something in your hand. Your fingers are wrapped tightly around it. You don't want to let go, no matter how many times you're told you should. So you keep it clutched in your fist.

It's time to let go, girl! Release those fingers one at a time. Now, take a close look. What's inside? What have you been holding on to? What? You've been hanging on to your worries and cares? Listen to God and let them go! Give them to the Lord! His hands are much bigger than yours, after all—and He wants to hold them for you.

Now wave your hands up in the air. Feel those worries lifting? Can you see them flying away? You were never meant to hold on to them in the first place, you know. God wants His daughters to live a worry-free life. So the next time you're tempted to worry, remember to open up those hands and let your troubles fly far, far away—into the hands of the Lord.

God, today I choose to let go of my worries and my cares!
I won't hold tight to them any longer. I release them to You!

SPEAK IT!

Then God said, "Let the water be filled with living things,
and let birds fly in the air above the earth."
GENESIS 1:20 NCV

. . . .

Isn't it interesting to think that God created the heavens and the earth just by speaking them into existence? Talk about amazing! And the very things He created—the rocks, rivers, trees, and so forth—all listened to the Lord's voice and obeyed! The rivers started flowing, the trees filled up with leaves, and the stars started twinkling!

What about you? What if you were asked to make a cake but were given no ingredients? No flour. No eggs. No oil. Nothing. Could you do it? Could you speak the word *cake* and expect one to miraculously appear? Of course not! Only God can perform miracles like that. But guess what? God really does want you to speak some miracles into existence.

"What sort of miracles?" you ask. Here's an example: When you're sad, God wants you to say, "The joy of the Lord is my strength!" Poof! Just speaking it will bring joy! When you're angry, He wants you to say, "I choose to forgive!" Poof! Just speaking the words helps you forgive the other person.

There is power in what you say, girl! So speak up! Then watch God move through your words.

. . . .

Father, what a great reminder that words have power.
You created the world with your words, and I can create
new situations with mine! I love it—and You!

THE WHOLE WIDE WORLD

*"For God so loved the world, that he gave his only Son,
that whoever believes in him should not perish
but have eternal life."*

JOHN 3:16 ESV

Do you ever stop to think about how huge planet Earth is? Seven continents. Hundreds of countries. Billions of people. Wow. It's overwhelming. There are so many different languages, so many different types of people. . . How does God keep up with us all? (Does He speak Swahili? French? Russian?)

It's hard to imagine that our Daddy God could love all of His kids—billions and billions of us—all the same amount. But it's true. Doesn't matter if you live in China, in Africa, or in the United States. God adores you! He's not worried about your skin color, how tall you are, what language you speak, or whether you live in a hut or a fancy house. He adores every person in the whole wide world.

Take a look at today's scripture. It's probably a very familiar one. The Lord has so much love for all of the people He created that He was willing to send His only Son to earth to die on a cross for their sins. He did that for all of us! What an amazing God we serve!

Lord, I'm blown away by how many people You created, but I'm even
more blown away when I think about how You love all of us
the same. Thank You for loving us that much.

FABULOUS IS AS FABULOUS DOES

Always be humble, gentle, and patient, accepting each other in love. You are joined together with peace through the Spirit, so make every effort to continue together in this way.

EPHESIANS 4:2–3 NCV

A lot of girls think they're fabulous because of the way they look or the cool clothes they wear. But the real test of fabulousness is on the inside. If you're truly fab, you will follow the instructions in today's scripture. You will be humble (not bragging about yourself or thinking you're better than others). You will be gentle (calm, cool, and collected). You will be patient (not always in a hurry to get your own way). You will accept one other in love (not judging others because of how they look or how they're different from you).

Here's the main thing: if you want to be totally fabulous, you have to learn how to live in peace with people around you. No squabbling with your brothers and sisters. No arguing with your friends at school. No talking back to your parents. No rolling your eyes behind your teacher's back.

So what do you think, girl? Can you do it? Your actions will be a reflection of your heart, so start by asking God for a totally fabulous heart, one that shines for Him!

God, I want to be fabulous, but I want to do it Your way.
Help me be humble, gentle, patient, and accepting.
Most of all, please help me to live in peace
with the people around me.

ENCOURAGERS

When Elizabeth heard Mary's greeting, her baby moved within her.
The Holy Spirit came upon Elizabeth. Then in a loud voice she said
to Mary: God has blessed you more than any other woman!
He has also blessed the child you will have.

LUKE 1:41–42 CEV

There's a really cool story in the New Testament about Mary, the mother of Jesus. She went to visit her cousin, Elizabeth, who was also expecting a baby. (Mommies-to-be love hanging out with one another, for sure!) Elizabeth said something amazing to Mary: "God has blessed you more than any other woman! He has also blessed the child you will have."

Wow! Now that's great news. Mary must've been so excited to hear that God was blessing her and her baby. And how sweet of Elizabeth to speak such great words to her. It must've taken a lot of love for her to say all of that to Mary. Talk about a terrific cousin!

Don't you just love people who speak encouraging words to you? They listen to the Lord's voice and then share what they hear with you so that your spirits can be lifted. These are the kinds of friends we need!

Do you want to be an encourager to others? Pray for them, and then share what good things the Lord is telling you! They will be so encouraged!

Lord, thank You for my encouraging friends.
They bless me! Please help me to be an encourager to others!

DON'T GIVE UP!

You never saw him, yet you love him. You still don't see him, yet you trust him—with laughter and singing. Because you kept on believing, you'll get what you're looking forward to: total salvation.

1 PETER 1:8–9 MSG

Imagine you were asked to climb a mountain. Do you think you could make it to the top? What if you made it halfway but got tired? Would you turn around and climb back down, never to finish the journey?

Sometimes it's tempting to give up, especially when life gets hard. But God says, "Don't stop! You can do it, even when things are tough!" No, it's not always easy, but with His help you can make it.

Need an example? Maybe you're taking ballet lessons, but things aren't going well. You can't seem to remember the different positions, and your feet get so mixed up every time the teacher asks you to perform. Maybe everyone brags about one of the other girls in the class. (Her feet seem to know exactly what to do!) She's so graceful, and you feel so clunky! You practice and practice but don't seem to be improving. Wouldn't it make more sense to quit while you're ahead?

Of course not! Winners never quit—and quitters never win! So keep on practicing! Don't give up.

Okay, Lord. . .I will keep going, even when I feel like giving up!
But I'm going to need Your help more than ever. Don't let me quit!

126

CRITICISM

I realize how kind God has been to me, and so I tell each of you not to think you are better than you really are. Use good sense and measure yourself by the amount of faith that God has given you.

ROMANS 12:3 CEV

Have you ever met someone who is critical of others? She's always cutting other people down and pointing out their flaws.

God doesn't like it when we're critical of others. We're not supposed to judge. Want to know why? First, because God is the only One who is sinless, so He's the only One worthy to judge anyone! Second, because we're just as sinful as the person we're judging.

Oh, you don't think you're sinful? You don't do wrong things? Take a look at today's verse. It says, "Use good sense and measure yourself by the amount of faith that God has given you." If we are really truly honest with ourselves, we have to admit that everyone, including us, makes mistakes. We all sin. We talk about people behind their backs, we have bad attitudes at times, and sometimes we talk back to our parents. In other words, we mess up. So we shouldn't be critical of others. We shouldn't think we're better than they are. Sure, they make mistakes, but we do too. God is kind and loving to us all—in spite of those mistakes! He's not pointing His finger at us, saying critical things. No way! He goes on loving us, no matter what.

Lord, I always seem to notice when other people make mistakes but sometimes ignore my own. Keep me humble. And help me to love others when they mess up, just as much as You love me when I mess up!

BITTERNESS

Let all bitterness and wrath and anger and clamor and slander be put away from you, along with all malice. Be kind to one another, tenderhearted, forgiving one another, as God in Christ forgave you.

EPHESIANS 4:31–32 ESV

Have you ever taken a bite of a piece of an orange, only to discover that it was really bitter? There's nothing worse than thinking you're eating something sweet, only to find out it's really sour. Ick!

The same thing can happen to people who are watching how we live as Christians. They think they're getting sweet fruit. And, sure, we act sweet most of the time, but sometimes we blow it by getting bitter (mad). Our friends who are watching think, *Wow! She's not so sweet after all! In fact, she's pretty sour!*

God wants us to put our bitterness away. No more sour fruit! He wants only sweet fruit hanging from His vine! If you're bearing sweet fruit, it means you treat others in a tender way. You forgive instead of holding a grudge. You show them the same loving-kindness that God has shown you. You never talk about them behind their back. In other words, you're not a sour person anymore! You're nothing but sweet, through and through!

God, I don't want to be a piece of bitter, sour fruit! I want to be sweet. When my friends spend time with me, I want them to know I'm Your child, filled with sweetness.

GOOD DEEDS

"In the same way, let your light shine before others, that they may see your good deeds and glorify your Father in heaven."

MATTHEW 5:16 NIV

Have you ever wondered how God expects you to shine your light for Him? You're not a car with headlights, after all! You're not a flashlight with a bright, shiny bulb! You're not a lamp on the bedside table.

The way that Christians shine their lights is by living holy lives in front of their friends. Doing this makes you so bright that your light shimmers and shines in the darkness.

So what is a holy life? To live in holiness means you're different from the crowd. You don't do the things everyone else is doing just so you can fit in. You care more about what God thinks than what your friends think. The more you please the Lord, the brighter you shine.

Shining your light also means that you care more about the needs of others than you do about your own. You want to reach out a helping hand to lift others up. Every time you do, you're shining your light, whether you realize it or not!

Father, I want to shine my light for You. I want to live a holy life and to care more about others than myself. Help me shimmer and shine!

A WRESTLING MATCH

You, LORD, give true peace to those who depend on you,
because they trust you. So, trust the LORD always,
because he is our Rock forever.

ISAIAH 26:3–4 NCV

Have you ever been to a wrestling match? Probably not. Still, if you've watched one on TV, you know that wrestlers are very large men, loaded with muscles and very, very strong. They put their trust in their own strength and try to take down their opponent.

We aren't as strong as wrestlers, are we? No way! We're not loaded with muscles like they are, and we definitely wouldn't have the courage to get in the ring for a wrestling match with someone who looked like Samson or Goliath! Still, when we put our trust in God, when we believe that He is fighting our battles for us, we're even stronger than the strongest wrestler. It's true! God's muscles are huge!

When we're trusting God to fight our battles for us, we don't have to worry about how strong—or how weak—we are. It doesn't matter. All that matters is *His* strength. He's the One who's doing the fighting, after all. So if you're facing an opponent today, don't be scared to climb into the ring. Just let God do the fighting. Trust Him to win the battle in His strength, not yours!

Oh Lord, I'm so glad You're the one fighting my battles.
I feel so weak and scrawny sometimes! You're the strong
One, Father! I'm so glad I can trust You!

130

BE YOURSELF

Do not be conformed to this world, but be transformed by the renewal of your mind, that by testing you may discern what is the will of God, what is good and acceptable and perfect.

ROMANS 12:2 ESV

Don't you love it when you're hanging out with people who encourage you to be yourself? You don't have to fake it around them! No sucking in your stomach. No acting like you're someone you're not. You can totally be yourself! Just plain you!

If you're ever caught up in a group of so-called friends who want you to pretend to be something you're not, run away as fast as you can! Those fakers aren't looking out for your best interests! They just want you to look like them and act like them so that they can appear more popular. They're not really interested in you. They just want to make themselves look good.

God created you to be unique—and you are. There's only one you. So why would you want to spend all of your time trying to fit into someone else's mold? The Lord is happiest when you look in the mirror and say, "You know what? I'm glad I'm me! I wouldn't want to be anyone else." That makes your Daddy God's heart very, very happy!

Lord, I'm the only "me" there is, and I know You made me just as I am.
I'm so glad I have the freedom to be myself. I don't have to
be like everyone else. I'm uniquely Yours!

LiFT IT uP!

Praise the LORD, my soul;
all my inmost being, praise his holy name.
PSALM 103:1 NIV

Praising God is a great way to change your thinking. Are you going through a tough time? If so, try lifting a song of praise to the King of kings and Lord of lords! That's right, sing! Doesn't matter what you're going through, a song of praise will help.

Maybe you have a hard time praising God when you're at home or riding your bike. Maybe you think that singing songs to Him should only happen at church or when you're listening to Christian music on the radio. But God wants you to sing, sing, sing every day! Why? Because praising lifts your spirits. It makes you focus on Him, not you, and that's always a good thing.

Sure, you should praise God when you're in church, but also praise Him when you're at home...even when things in your life aren't going great. When you're having an icky day or feeling sick, sing out a praise song and watch your Daddy God lift your spirits and make your day much, much better!

Heavenly Father, I confess I don't always feel like praising.
Some days I just feel blah. On those icky days, please remind me
that praise is powerful! That it will help me get past the bad
stuff and remind me that You are in control.

I WiLL NOT BE SHAKEN

I know the LORD is always with me.
I will not be shaken, for he is right beside me.

PSALM 16:8 NLT

What does it mean to "be shaken"? Does it mean you stand in the room, trembling all over? Not necessarily. To be shaken might mean that you get blown off course during a rough season and lose your way. You lose your confidence and feel lost.

Here's an example: Imagine everything is going well, and then your dad gets really sick. He has to go in the hospital. He can't work anymore, and you can tell that your mom is really worried. What do you do? Do you let this storm blow you off course, or do you hold tight to your faith in God, believing that He will work it all out in the end?

Some situations are really scary and we do get shaken, but we don't have to stay that way. Just go to God and say, "Lord, I'm scared!" Then ask Him to remind You that He is in control and is standing right beside you. Your shaky season won't last forever—that's a promise!

Lord, I get so scared sometimes. When bad things happen, I tend to worry.
Thank You for reminding me that shaky seasons don't last forever
and that You are so near I can reach out and touch You!

DECISION MAKING

Always let him lead you, and he will clear
the road for you to follow.
PROVERBS 3:6 CEV

Decisions, decisions! How do we make big decisions? Do we play the eenie-meenie-miney-moe game? Do we ask our friends for their advice? Do we draw straws?

Whenever you have a big decision to make, there's really only one way to handle it—you need to pray and ask God for His opinion. He will give it! Oh, He probably won't speak in a big, booming voice, but He will let you know in your heart which direction to go. He won't leave you feeling lost and alone.

So what decisions are you facing today? Are you wondering if you should be friends with the new girl at school? Are you trying to decide if you should take a certain class at school? Thinking about signing up for music lessons or ballet class? Yes, life is filled with decisions, but you can make the right ones with God's help. Just ask Him today. He'll not only let you know what to do. He'll clear the way for you! Simply listen for His still, small voice in your heart.

Father, I'm listening! I have some decisions to make
and I need Your help. No more eenie-meenie-miney-moe for me!
From now on I listen for Your still, small voice!

BAD LANGUAGE

Stop all your dirty talk. Say the right thing at the right time and help others by what you say.
EPHESIANS 4:29 CEV

Have you ever been around people who used bad language? Sounds icky, doesn't it? Using bad language (cussing) isn't a sign of being cool or popular—it's just plain awful. God doesn't like dirty words, and it breaks His heart when His kids use them! Don't believe it? Check out today's scripture: "Stop all your dirty talk." That makes it pretty obvious that God doesn't like it!

One of the main reasons bad language is icky is because it ruins your testimony. Your *testimony* is the story of what God has done in your life, how He has changed your heart. Imagine you've told your friend that you love Jesus. You've even invited her to church. Then you start using really bad language. Your friend will probably say, "But I thought she was a Christian. Why is she talking like that?"

See the point? If you say you're a Christian, you need to act like one! People are watching. So no bad language. It's not cool, and it's definitely not something God likes. Wash that mouth out with spiritual soap, and make up your mind to use only nice words from now on!

God, I don't want to break Your heart, and I don't want to mess up my testimony. Please keep me from using dirty words. I want to honor You, Lord.

FOLLOW WHERE HE LEADS

"Before I finished praying in my heart, Rebekah came out,
with her jar on her shoulder. She went down to the spring
and drew water, and I said to her, 'Please give me a drink.'"
GENESIS 24:45 NIV

There's a really cool story in the Old Testament about a young woman named Rebekah. She went to the well to get some water, never knowing that her life would change in that instant! At the well she met a man who told her that she was going to get married. Wow. She probably never saw that one coming!

Did you know that God still speaks to us today? When we follow His leading and go to the places He wants us to go, He will meet us there and speak to our hearts. Here's an example: Maybe you aren't sure if you want to go to church camp. You feel a little nudging from God to go, so you go (even though it's hard to leave Mom and Dad). While you're at camp, you have an awesome time and ask Jesus to come live in your heart. Your whole life is changed because you listened and followed God's leading.

See? When we follow God to the places He leads, He speaks and changes our lives, just like He did with Rebekah!

Father, thank You for the life-changing encounters I've had.
I will gladly follow wherever You lead!

PHOTO ALBUMS

Direct your children onto the right path, and
when they are older, they will not leave it.

PROVERBS 22:6 NLT

Don't you love looking at pictures? Back in the "old days," people kept wonderful photo albums (special books with pictures inside). Maybe your parents or grandparents have some albums you can look through. These days people keep their pictures on the computer, their phone, even in digital picture frames. Doesn't matter where you keep them, it's just a good idea to have them so that you never forget the very special lives of your parents, grandparents, aunts, uncles, and so forth.

Why is it so fun to look at pictures of family members (say, a picture of your mom when she was a little girl)? Your family is a part of you, after all! When you see that picture of your mom, you're reminded that you are a part of something bigger than yourself. It's also easy to see how God has brought your family from one generation to another.

Just think! One day your children will look at pictures of you as a little girl. They will say, "Mommy, look how cute you were! I love your curls! I love your funny-looking little outfit!" What fun that will be!

Lord, thank You for giving me pictures to look at. I'm so happy
that I'm part of a bigger family. And I can't wait to see
what I look like when I'm all grown up!

HEAVEN

"My Father's house has many rooms; if that were not so,
would I have told you that I am going there
to prepare a place for you?"

JOHN 14:2 NIV

. . . .

Do you ever think about heaven? Do you realize that you will have a mansion (a huge house) when you get there? This won't be any ordinary house! It's going to be more amazing than any house on earth, and the street in front of it will be paved in gold. Yep, gold!

Here on earth we often have struggles. We don't get to see God's full plan for our lives. But when we get to heaven, there will be no more pain, no more sorrow (no tears!), no more weakness. In heaven, everything will be wonderful! You won't have anything to whine or complain about, that's for sure! You'll be too busy worshipping God and singing with the angels to complain, anyway.

If you're having a bad day today, just close your eyes and think about what heaven will be like. The troubles of today will pass away. One day we will all be together in that amazing place with streets of gold!

. . . .

Father, sometimes I get too worked up about the problems I face and
I forget that one day I will be in heaven with You. When I'm having
a tough day, please remind me that I will spend eternity
with You, walking down golden streets!

BIBLE PROMISES

For all the promises of God in [Jesus] are Yes,
and in Him Amen, to the glory of God through us.
2 CORINTHIANS 1:20 NKJV

. . . .

Did you know that the Bible is loaded with promises? It's true! God has promised His kids lots of things: He won't ever leave us or forsake us (see Hebrews 13:5). He listens to our prayers (see Psalm 116:1). He won't let us down (see Isaiah 26:4). He heals people's diseases (see Psalm 103:3). He gives us wisdom (see Proverbs 1:7). God is all-powerful (Psalm 62:11). God takes away our fears (see Psalm 23:4). We can be joyful, even in hard times (see Philippians 4:4).

We could spend all day talking about the promises of God, but here's the point: He won't ever let us down! No way! We serve a God who doesn't go back on His promises. If He has said it, He will do it. Sure, people let us down sometimes, but the Lord never will. We can place our trust in His Word. What an amazing God we serve!

. . . .

Lord, sometimes it hurts my feelings when people go back on their promises. I'm so glad that You never will! If You say it, You will do it!

WORSHIP ONLY GOD

When the people saw that Moses was so long in coming down from the mountain, they gathered around Aaron and said, "Come, make us gods who will go before us. As for this fellow Moses who brought us up out of Egypt, we don't know what has happened to him."

EXODUS 32:1 NIV

There's an interesting story in the Old Testament about a group of people (the Israelites) who turned their back on God. Oh, they believed in Him for a while; then they changed their minds and started worshipping a golden calf! Can you believe it? Why in the world would they worship a goofy-looking thing like that?

Might sound ridiculous to us, but these days we sometimes spend too much time playing video games or watching TV—other things that steal our time. Might not be the same thing as worshipping a golden calf, but if we're not careful, we can find ourselves giving all of our attention to these things when we should be focused on God and others.

So what's *your* golden calf? Do you have something that you've made a little too important? Your clothes? Your money? Your computer? Your television shows? Your friendships? Make sure you're worshipping God, not "stuff."

Father, thanks for the reminder that my stuff shouldn't be as important to me as You! No golden calves for me! My heart worships You alone!

FiNDiNG VALUE iN PEOPLE, NOT THiNGS

"Fear not, therefore; you are of more value than many sparrows."
MATTHEW 10:31 ESV

Have you ever been to a fancy jewelry store? If so, then you've seen some really expensive necklaces, rings, and bracelets. All around us, people put value in their "stuff"—houses, cars, clothes, handbags, shoes, and so on. You might think, *Well, I don't have a lot of money, so I don't own a lot of stuff.* Is that so? You have clothes, shoes, toys, and all sorts of things, right? Just make sure you don't value them more than the people in your life!

Imagine you wanted to buy a really special toy. You saved and saved until you had the money to buy it. All you talked about, night and day, was that toy. You went on and on and on, talking about how one day you would own it. Finally the day came and you bought the toy! Yay! It meant the world to you. Only one problem. . . You were so busy thinking about that toy that you forgot about your friends, your parents, your brothers and sisters, and so on. You had made the toy the most important thing in your life.

This might seem like a silly example, but we do things like this all the time. So be careful. Remember that God wants us to find value in people, not our toys.

Thanks for the reminder, Lord! My stuff isn't valuable to me—people are!
I love my friends and family so much more than my toys!

JOY IN THE MORNING

Crying may last for a night, but joy comes in the morning.
PSALM 30:5 NCV

Ever had a really rough night? Maybe you stayed up until the wee hours, crying your eyes out over something that really upset you. Maybe your best friend said something to hurt your feelings, or maybe you were angry at your parents or little brother about something. So you stayed up half the night, crying and worrying.

There's good news! If you can just fall asleep on nights like that, you will awaken in the morning with a new outlook on life! With the sunrise comes a brand-new day—and a happier one at that! All of those troubles that loomed large in the night don't seem so important the next morning, that's for sure! So the next time it looks like it's going to be a rough night, forget about crying your eyes out. Instead, wipe away all those tears. Remember, God promises that joy will come in the morning. So get some rest and start fresh tomorrow.

Father, sometimes I have a hard time falling asleep because I'm upset about things. My feelings are hurt or I'm worried or angry. Help me to sleep tight and wake up in the morning, refreshed and ready to start a new day.

THE RAINBOW AFTER A STORM

"I will set My rain-bow in the cloud, and it will be something special to see because of an agreement between Me and the earth."
GENESIS 9:13 NLV

If you've ever looked up in the sky after a rainstorm to discover a brilliant rainbow with all of its bright colors, then you know what hope feels like. You really can go on after life's storms, even when it feels impossible. The rainbow is a sign, a colorful bow of hope. It says to you, "Hey! You can keep going! I know it's been hard, but don't give up! Remember Noah? Remember the flood? Even after such a difficult storm, Noah kept going and ended up on dry land."

We all go through stormy seasons, whether we're kids or adults. God won't forget you when you're going through a hard time. If you ever doubt that, just look up at the rainbow and you will be reminded that tomorrow will be a much brighter day.

Trust God. He will never ever let you down. That's His promise.

God, sometimes I need a reminder that tomorrow will be better than today!
I'll bet Noah needed that reminder when he was on the ark too!
Thanks for the rainbow, Lord! It gives me hope.

Turning My Sorrow to Dancing

*You changed my sorrow into dancing. You took away my
clothes of sadness, and clothed me in happiness.*

PSALM 30:11 NCV

If you've ever been really, really sad, you know how hard it is to snap out of it. What if you could be really sad one minute and dancing for joy the next? Seem impossible? It's not! The Bible says that God can turn our mourning (sadness) into dancing. How does this happen? You have to go to Him when you're sad. Open up your hands and say, "Here, Lord! I don't want this anymore." He will take it right then and there.

And turning your troubles over to God isn't as hard as you might think, either. Get alone with Him. Be honest. Say, "Lord, I'm really struggling. Help me, please!" He will. Pour your heart out, girl! Tell Him exactly what's troubling you. As you give your troubles to Him (and that's what He wants you to do), you will feel a hundred pounds lighter! Before long your toes will be tapping and your heart will be ready to burst into a happy song.

You won't even remember the sadness and troubles of yesterday once the dance begins.

Father, I want to let go of my sadness and troubles. I would much rather
dance a jig than have a crying jag! I give my griefs to You,
Lord. Please replace my sorrow with dancing!

144

A BUBBLY PERSONALITY

Rejoice always, pray continually, give thanks in all circumstances;
for this is God's will for you in Christ Jesus.
1 Thessalonians 5:16–18 niv

Have you ever met someone who just seemed to bubble, bubble, bubble with God's joy? Maybe she reminded you of a fountain, always spraying water all over the place! Talk about contagious joy!

Maybe she couldn't stop giggling or always had a smile on her face! Maybe she laughed loud and long! Maybe she told funny jokes and made everyone chuckle. Regardless, she just kept bubbling over, day after day!

Sure, girls like that may seem a little goofy—or even silly—at times, but in the long run, they keep your spirits up and always see the glass as half full. They're not faking it. No way! They really, truly trust God and know that things are going to work out okay in the end. Their joy is the real deal, bubbling over like a water fountain.

Are you a bubbly girl? If not, you could pray about it and ask God to help you. He will give you His joy, which will bubble up inside of your heart and make everything seem better!

Father, I know some bubbly girls who seem very joyful.
I want to bubble with Your joy too. Can You fill me up like a fountain?

LEAH

When morning came, there was Leah! So Jacob said to Laban,
"What is this you have done to me? I served you for
Rachel, didn't I? Why have you deceived me?"
GENESIS 29:25 NIV

Poor Leah! What a hard life she had. You can read her story in Genesis 29. Her father played a mean trick on a man named Jacob and used Leah as part of that trick. Jacob thought he was marrying Leah's younger sister, Rachel, but he married Leah instead. (Hey, you think you've got it bad sometimes? At least your father hasn't used you to fool someone else!)

Whenever really rotten things happen to us, especially when we're hurt badly by someone we love, we have to learn to forgive. If we don't choose to forgive the person for what he or she did, bitterness will grow in our heart. Before long we'll be cranky and mean to *everyone*—and all because we didn't forgive one person.

Has someone you loved hurt you? If so, don't grow bitter. Instead, get better! Forgive. Release the person by saying, "God, I don't understand why she did that to me, but I choose to forgive anyway." There! Doesn't that feel better?

Father, I don't always understand why people hurt others. It really stinks
to be hurt by someone you loved and trusted. But I choose to forgive,
Lord. I won't look back, and I won't grow bitter. I'll only get better!

ADVICE FROM MAMA

One generation shall praise Your works to another,
and shall declare Your mighty acts.

PSALM 145:4 NASB

One of the coolest things about having a mom, a grandma, or an aunt is this: you can go to her for advice. The women in your life are very wise! They've lived a long time and have lots to share. They can teach you all sorts of things—how to cook, how to love others, how to live a fun-filled life!

Sure, you're a kid. You want to hang around other girls your own age. But don't forget that God has placed the older women in your life for a reason. They are there to share their experience with you and to help you grow into a godly woman, just like them. So next time you need some advice, when you don't know what to do, seek out your mom. Or your grandma. Or an elderly neighbor. These women will fill you up with great advice and give you a good dose of love at the very same time. Now that's a win-win situation, girl!

Lord, thank You for the women in my life. I love getting their advice
and hearing their stories. These women are so full of
wisdom! I'm so grateful for their loving hearts!

THE NARROW PATH

*"Strive to enter through the narrow door.
For many, I tell you, will seek to enter
and will not be able."*

LUKE 13:24 ESV

Imagine going for a walk in the woods. You find a long skinny trail and follow it, going deeper into the forest. After a while, the path gets really narrow. . . so narrow that you can barely keep going. What will you do? Give up? Turn around? Go another way? Stick to the narrow path?

Following God is a lot like that path. It's a narrow road. Not many people find it, and those who do sometimes get discouraged and head off down a different path, one that seems easier.

Not you, though! You keep walking down that narrow road, girl! That's the road God wants you on. He will show you the way, so trust Him. Don't follow others who want to go a different direction. They're just going to get lost anyway! You stick with God. The journey might not always be easy, but it will be worth it in the end.

God, I don't want to follow my friends; I want to follow You!
Sure, the trail is narrow at times. And it's not
always easy. But it's so worth it!

SEARCH AND SEE!

*Dear friend, take my advice; it will add years to your life.
I'm writing out clear directions to Wisdom Way,
I'm drawing a map to Righteous Road.*

PROVERBS 4:10–11 MSG

Imagine you stumbled across a treasure map. Wow! You would follow all of the clues until you found the hidden treasure, wouldn't you? Of course. And the treasure would mean so much to you, no matter what kind of riches you found inside the box.

Did you know that the kingdom of heaven is like a treasure? We search and search to discover the little jewels (love, faith, peace, joy, and so on) that God has for us. They're all in that treasure box, just waiting to be taken out.

So what are you waiting for, girl? Start hunting! Pray and ask the Lord to reveal the hidden treasures to you. He will lead you down a road to all sorts of great surprises that will change your life. Discovering God's treasures is a grand adventure, one that you will never regret. So grab that map! Start hunting!

Father, thank You for showing me that my journey with You
is like following a treasure map. You are leading me to
discover amazing jewels every step of the way!

SETTING GOALS

"For which of you, desiring to build a tower, does not first sit down and count the cost, whether he has enough to complete it?"

LUKE 14:28 ESV

Are you a goal setter? Do you plan out your day or make lists? If not, you might want to try it, because it's important to set goals, even small ones. Your chances of hitting the target are much better if you are actually aiming for it! Goals are an awesome way to keep your life moving toward a happy destination.

So how do you set goals, anyway? First of all, pray and ask God to give you goals. Maybe He wants you to save a certain amount of money to help support a child in another country. You set a goal of thirty dollars. Then pray and ask God to give you a strategy to raise the money. Maybe you can earn ten dollars cleaning house for a neighbor, then another ten dollars babysitting. Maybe the final ten dollars can come from selling lemonade at a lemonade stand.

The point is, God will show you how to work your way toward your destination, one step at a time. No, it won't all happen in one day. It takes patience to work your way toward a goal. But if you don't give up, you will make it, one step at a time. And, oh, what amazing lessons you will learn along the way!

Father, thank You for giving me goals! I want to do great things for You! Help me figure out what to do; then give me the strategies to do it, one day at a time!

LOYALTY

A man of many companions may come to ruin,
but there is a friend who sticks closer than a brother.
PROVERBS 18:24 ESV

What does it mean to be loyal? A loyal person is someone who sticks with you, even when it's hard. If you're a loyal friend, you don't give up on the friendship, even when problems come up. (And let's face it, all friendships go through hard times!) To be loyal means you have a stick-with-it attitude.

Not everyone is loyal, of course. Some people won't want to hang around for long. They act like they're your friend one day then disappear the next. You can't really control all of that, but you can control the kind of friend you will be to others. So make up your mind. Say to yourself, "I'm going to be the kind of friend who doesn't give up, even when it's tough."

God will reward your faithfulness. He knows what it's like to be a loyal friend. After all, He has stayed close to you every day of your life and doesn't plan on ever leaving you, no matter how many mistakes you make. Talk about loyalty! So learn from God! You won't find a better teacher!

Father, You are a loyal friend to me! I too want to be a loyal friend
to others, not giving up on friendships when they
get hard. Teach me how to do this, Lord.

FIGHT THE GOOD FIGHT

Fight the good fight of faith, grabbing hold of the life that continues forever. You were called to have that life when you confessed the good confession before many witnesses.

1 TIMOTHY 6:12 NCV

Have you ever gotten into a fight with a friend, brother, or sister? Fights aren't much fun, are they? Sooner or later one person says something rude and another person ends up getting her feelings hurt. And what's the fight about, anyway? Usually it's about something goofy, something that doesn't really matter anyway.

If you have to fight, why not fight "the good fight." That's what the Bible calls our faith journey. The "good fight" is the life we live as Christians. We battle a lot of enemies (laziness, jealousy, and other things that mess us up). But we can win the battle if we don't give up.

So how do we fight the good fight? We take up our weapons: love, faith, gentleness, self-control, patience. . . These and many more can be used to fight off the enemies of anger, impatience, frustration, and so on. We battle using the Sword of the Spirit (God's Word), and we keep on fighting to win the good fight, no matter how hard! Girl, this is one battle you are going to walk away from in triumph!

Father, I want to be a winner in the good fight of faith.
Show me the weapons that I need to get the job done!

152

A House on the Rock

"Everyone then who hears these words of mine and does them will be like a wise man who built his house on the rock. And the rain fell, and the floods came, and the winds blew and beat on that house, but it did not fall, because it had been founded on the rock."

MATTHEW 7:24–25 ESV

Obeying God is so important! If you read today's scripture, you can see that obedience is kind of like building a house on rock. It's a wise thing to do! When you ignore the words in the Bible and do your own thing, it's like building a house on the sand. The waters come along and wash it away! That's not a very solid foundation, is it?

So which would you like—a house built on the rock or a house on the sand? The rock, of course! But once your house is on that rock-solid foundation, how do you keep it there? By following the rules of the Bible. By reading God's Word and praying every day.

So don't follow after your friends, doing the things they do that might pull you away from God. Instead, keep your eyes on Jesus and your feet off the shifting sand!

You *can* be strong in Christ and stay rock solid. . .just obey!

Father, I get it! I can have a house on the rock if I follow the Bible and pray. I won't slip and slide like so many of my friends do. No on-the-sand houses for me! I'm going to stay built on You, the Rock!

THE GOOD SAMARITAN

Then a Samaritan traveling down the road came to where the hurt man was. When he saw the man, he felt very sorry for him.

LUKE 10:33 NCV

Have you ever read the story in the Bible about the Good Samaritan? A certain man was beaten up and badly injured by robbers. He was left to die on the side of the road. Several religious people passed by and left him on the street. (Can you imagine? How mean!) Then along came a Samaritan. Now, the Samaritans weren't usually known as being the good guys, but this one was. He saw the poor man and stopped to help. The Samaritan paid for the injured man to stay in a hotel while he recovered and made sure he had everything he needed while getting better.

Sometimes we judge people before we get to know them. The very people we think might be bad are sometimes good, and the people we think are good sometimes turn out to be bad! That's why we have to give all people a chance. Don't be so quick to judge whether someone is good or not. It's not your place to decide that, anyway. Only God can see inside the heart! And what He sees just might surprise you!

Lord, I know that sometimes I decide to judge people when I shouldn't.
Help me see that everyone deserves a chance, especially
those who are different from me.

MADE FROM A RIB

While the man slept, the LORD God took out one of the man's ribs
and closed up the opening. Then the LORD God made a
woman from the rib, and he brought her to the man.

GENESIS 2:21–22 NLT

Did you ever wonder why God decided to make men and women? Why not just one or the other?

The Lord created man first (Adam) and placed him in the Garden of Eden. After that God decided Adam needed a friend. So while Adam was sleeping, God took one of the man's ribs and made a woman.

Think about that for a minute. Women were created out of a rib. God didn't pick one of Adam's ankle bones so that men could stomp on women! He didn't pick a bone from Adam's head so that the woman would be the ruler, the one making all the decisions in the relationship. He picked a bone near Adam's heart because He knew that Eve would fall in love with Adam and they would have a family together. Sweet, right?

Isn't that a cool story of how women were created? We were made to fall in love, get married, and have families. And we were also created to fall in love with God who is our Creator. He's the One who designed us, after all, and He holds us close to His heart. No, we don't live in the Garden of Eden, but one day we will live in heaven, which is going to be even more beautiful!

Lord, I get it! You created women after men, but that doesn't mean You love us less! Maybe You saved the best for last, Father! I'm so excited that You chose to create me and that You hold me close to Your heart.

THE PRODIGAL SON

"So he got up and went to his father. But while he was still a long way off,
his father saw him and was filled with compassion for him; he ran
to his son, threw his arms around him and kissed him."

LUKE 15:20 NIV

Jesus told a really interesting story about two brothers. The younger one made a random decision to leave his father's house and try living on his own. He said, "Hey, Dad, please give me my share of the inheritance. I'm going away for a while." The father gave him the inheritance (a large sum of money). The younger brother went away and blew all the money! He spent it on goofy things and ended up living in the gutter with the pigs. (Ick!)

All this time the older brother stayed home and worked for the father, doing the good things that a son should do. In the end, the younger brother came home and said, "Dad, I messed up! I'm so sorry. Please let me come back home. You don't have to welcome me as a son. I'm okay just being a servant in your household." But the father greeted him with open arms and even threw a party to welcome the prodigal (reckless one) back to the family!

Sometimes we're like the younger son. We wander away from God, do our own thing, then come back home, sorry we messed up. Isn't it great to know our Father welcomes us back?

Lord, sometimes I mess up! I'm like the prodigal son. I'm so grateful that You take me back and forgive me! Thank You for being the best Dad ever.

NOTHING IS IMPOSSIBLE!

"For nothing is impossible with God."
LUKE 1:37 NLT

So many times we face obstacles that seem impossible. We think we'll never make it through. Here's great news, girl! *Nothing* is impossible with God. That's right—absolutely nothing. If you really believed that, it would change the way you pray, the things you say, and the people you hang out with. If nothing is impossible with God, you can believe Him when you ask for miracles.

So what miracle does your family need today? Are things rough? Are people going through sickness? Does your dad need a job? Is your grandpa having surgery? No matter how tough things seem, you can look up to heaven with a song in your heart. Lift your arms and cry out, asking God to do the impossible. The Bible says that He delights in doing impossible things. That means He really, really loves doing them! They bring joy to His heart.

Start believing God for big, impossible things. He's waiting to hear your requests. Don't be afraid to ask, girl!

Father, sometimes I'm afraid to ask for miracles.
They seem so. . .impossible! It helps a lot to know that You
delight in doing the impossible. I'm going to ask, Lord!

Who Is My Neighbor?

" 'You shall love the Lord your God with all your heart, and with all your soul, and with all your mind.' This is the great and foremost commandment. The second is like it, 'You shall love your neighbor as yourself.' "

MATTHEW 22:37–39 NASB

Take a close look at today's Bible verse. It's very interesting, isn't it? You might read this and say, "I do love God, but I can't figure out the 'neighbor' part. Who is my neighbor, anyway? Is it the elderly man who lives next door? Is it the little girl and her parents who live across the street?"

When God talks about us loving our neighbor, He's not just talking about the people who live next to us; He's talking about all of the people with whom we go to school, take gymnastics, study, eat, play, and so on. Our neighbors are the people we "do life" with. God wants us to love each one of them unconditionally.

The next time you read a verse about your neighbor, remember it's not just talking about the lady next door!

Lord, I get it! My neighbor isn't just the guy across the street. It's not just the kids next door. My neighbors are all around me! I see them every day!

158

BRAGGER!

*May the proud be ashamed, because they do wrong to me
for no reason, but I will think about Your Law.*
PSALM 119:78 NLV

Have you ever known someone who liked to brag? Maybe she went on and on and on about how talented she was, or maybe she liked to boast about her good grades. Braggers can wear you out in a hurry! They make you want to put cotton balls in your ears so you don't have to listen!

So how does God feel about bragging? He's not keen on it, for sure! The Bible says that we are to be humble. To be humble means you don't think too highly of yourself. You don't go around bragging about how you're better at this or that than other people. You see that other people are talented, smart, and kind, and you care more about making a big deal out of them than yourself.

The next time you're around someone who brags, brags, brags, be careful not to join in, boasting about yourself. Just learn from her mistake and stay humble. Maybe she'll learn a few lessons from you.

God, I don't want to be a bragger. I don't want to look like a show-off.
Help me to watch what I say about myself so that
I don't come across as being prideful!

A RAINY DAY

*Again he prayed, and the heavens gave rain,
and the earth produced its crops.*
JAMES 5:18 NIV

The earth needs rain for the crops to grow and for the trees and grass to be healthy. Instead of groaning and moaning when rainy days come, think of all the fun things you can do on this very special day!

Did you know that some people love the rain? It's true! Rainy days aren't as boring as you might think. In fact, some girls enjoy the pitter-patter of raindrops on the rooftop. They find it comforting. They're especially happy when it rains while they're in bed sleeping. They're not scared, not at all!

What about you? Do you enjoy the rain? If so, then you can spend the next rainy day curled up with a good book or a sewing project. One great thing about the rain is that it forces you to stay indoors with others. Maybe you could play board games or watch a movie with your mom. The best thing of all might be to rest!

Dear Lord, thank You for the lovely rain. It makes everything grow.
And it gives me the chance to stay inside and spend
time with my family. Sweet!

GiVE It AWAY

In her deep anguish Hannah prayed to the Lord,
weeping bitterly.
1 Samuel 1:10 niv

There's a really cool story in the Old Testament about a woman named Hannah. She desperately wanted to have a baby but wasn't able to. So she promised God that if He gave her a son, she'd give the boy back to Him. Finally, after praying and praying, Hannah had a son. She named him Samuel. When Samuel was just a tiny boy, she took him to the temple and told the priest, "I want you to raise him in the temple." Wow! After waiting so long for a baby, she had to give him up? Can you imagine how hard that must've been?

Maybe you can imagine. Maybe you've had a dream. You've wished for something. . .let's say a computer. You waited and waited and finally God gave you a really cool computer. Then, after that, something happened to your dad's computer and he had to start using yours because he couldn't afford to buy another one.

Ouch! See how hard it would be to give your heart's desire away after waiting for it for so long? But God will honor this kind of sacrifice. In Hannah's case he blessed her! Samuel grew up to be a mighty man of God, one who made his mama very, very proud!

Lord, I want to be the kind of girl who is willing to let go of things,
even the things I really, really want. Help me to be generous like Hannah!

LOVE NEVER FAILS

Love never gives up, never loses faith, is always hopeful,
and endures through every circumstance.

1 CORINTHIANS 13:7 NLT

What does it mean to give up? It means you quit! You've had it! You're not doing it anymore. What if God decided to give up on you? That would be awful, wouldn't it? Here's the truth: God's love never gives up. Never. Ever. No matter what.

So what about us? Are we supposed to love others in a never-give-up sort of way? You betcha! The kind of love that God expects from us is the kind that goes the distance. It keeps going and going, no matter what. And that's not all! The kind of love that God expects from His girls is the kind that doesn't get angry. It isn't jealous. It's not puffed up. It puts others first. Is not selfish! This special kind of love is quick to forgive and doesn't hold a grudge. It's also very happy with the truth. Wow! That's a very miraculous kind of love, isn't it?

Does it sound impossible? With God's help, all things are possible, even never-ending love!

Lord, please show me how to love others with a never-give-up attitude. I'm not a quitter, Father! Help me to keep loving, even when I don't feel like it.

MARY, THE MOTHER OF JESUS

And Mary said, "My soul magnifies the Lord,
and my spirit rejoices in God my Savior."
LUKE 1:46–47 ESV

Have you ever heard the story of Mary, the mother of Baby Jesus? Maybe at Christmastime you've listened to people talk about her, how she gave birth to our Savior. Here's the truth: Mary was just a young woman when the angel told her that she was going to have a baby, and she wasn't even married yet. Can you imagine how scared she was? It was probably pretty shocking to have an angel talk to her in the first place! But to find out she was going to have a baby? Wow! That's not something you hear every day, now, is it?

God gave her a huge task—to give birth to the Savior of the world. Just an ordinary young woman, but such a big thing to do! She didn't panic, though. No way. She trusted God, and He used her to change the world! Maybe He wants to do something remarkable with your life too!

Dear Lord, I want to have the faith of Mary! I want to hear Your voice
and trust You for huge things! Mary had a big test of faith,
and she passed it. May it be so with me!

LOAVES AND FISHES

And my God will meet all your needs according
to the riches of his glory in Christ Jesus.
PHILIPPIANS 4:19 NIV

There's a wonderful story in the New Testament that will give you faith to believe that God definitely works miracles! Five thousand people had gathered to hear Jesus teach. After a while their tummies started to growl. Talk about hungry! These folks were starving! Only one problem—none of the grown-ups had packed a lunch.

One little boy had a sack lunch. He had five loaves of bread and two fish. He probably didn't plan to share it with five thousand people, but that's just what happened. After thanking God for the boy's food, Jesus told His disciples to take the five loaves and two fishes and to share them among the people. Lo and behold, the food kept multiplying. . .and multiplying. . .and multiplying! There was plenty to feed everyone, with lots of food left over afterward. Wow! God is definitely in the multiplying business! What an awesome provider He is!

Father, wow! You took five loaves of bread and two little fish and fed five thousand people? That's amazing! If You cared enough about those people to give them lunch, then I know You will take care of my needs too!

THE WIDOW'S OFFERING

He said, "I tell you the truth, this poor woman has put in more than
all of them. For they have put in a little of the money they had
no need for. She is very poor and has put in all she had.
She has put in what she needed for her own living."

LUKE 21:3–4 NLV

Some people have a lot of money and don't mind giving some of it away to help others in need. Some are a little stingy. They have the money but don't feel like helping out. And then there are people like the lady in today's story. She didn't have much money at all, but guess what she did with the little bit she did have—she gave it all away! That's right! She put all of her money into the offering to help people in need.

Wow. Think about that for a minute. She didn't just give away a dollar or two. She reached into her pocket and brought out everything she had then dropped it all in the offering. Could you do that? Could you empty your piggy bank and put everything in the offering? It would be hard, right?

When you trust God to provide all that you need, you have faith enough to give like this woman did. Jesus definitely loved her giving heart.

Lord, I'm so impressed with this woman who gave everything she had.
What faith! Help me to be more generous with my giving,
Father. May I learn a lesson from this sweet lady!

WHO IS THE GREATEST?

"Let the greatest among you be as the least.
Let the leader be as the one who cares for others."
LUKE 22:26 NLV

Think of the most powerful person you know. Maybe she's a famous singer or an amazing actress from Hollywood. Maybe he's a great politician or a popular author. The point is, some people seem to have everything. Their every wish comes true! They're very famous and popular. Everyone thinks they're great. But. . .are they? Really?

How does God feel about popularity? Does He care who's the greatest in any special field? Not really. He's more impressed with the people who quietly help others. He loves it when you read a book to an elderly neighbor or obey your parents without being asked twice. These are the things that make you great in God's eyes!

So which would you rather be—great in the eyes of the world or great in the eyes of the Lord?

Lord, thank You for the reminder that You don't look at the most
popular person and say, "Wow, she's awesome!" Instead,
You're impressed by how and when I help others.

A HEART FILLED WITH COMPASSION

But you, O Lord, are a God of compassion and mercy,
slow to get angry and filled with unfailing love and faithfulness.
PSALM 86:15 NLT

Are you a compassionate girl? If so, that means your heart goes out to those in need. You feel sympathetic when you see a sick child in the hospital. A homeless man on the street corner, begging for food. The girl at school whom no one wants to be friends with. When you're compassionate, it truly hurts your heart to see others in pain. You can hardly stand it.

Here's the good news: if you're compassionate, you are definitely not alone. God is also very compassionate. Read today's scripture one more time. If you want to be more like the Lord, adopt His version of compassion: be slow to anger and show mercy to others, especially those in need.

Being compassionate isn't a sign of weakness. In fact, it's just the opposite. When your heart goes out to people who are hurting, it shows that you are very strong. You're also becoming more like the Lord every time you reach out to help others—so you go, girl!

Lord, I want to be compassionate like You. Show me how to help
people in need, using a warm, loving heart and a calm mind.

BRINGING JOY TO HIS HEART

He received honor and glory from God the Father when
the voice came to him from the Majestic Glory, saying,
"This is my Son, whom I love; with him I am well pleased."

2 PETER 1:17 NIV

Imagine a young princess in the throne room, sitting at her father's feet while he rules the kingdom. She loves sitting there, looking up at him with stars in her eyes. Her daddy loves it too. He knows how much she loves him, and that makes his heart so glad!

Now imagine the king in that story is your Daddy God. Like your earthly parents, God loves everything about you. He loved watching when you learned to walk, and He celebrated when you learned to play patty-cake. He has been there for every victory, cheering you on. Through your ups and your downs, He's been watching—and smiling.

God is especially pleased when you obey your parents and the other adults in your life. That really makes Him happy! He loves it when you do the right thing, even without being asked (like doing homework without having to be reminded). Why? Because it shows Him that you are learning. You're growing. And while you're doing that, continue to love your heavenly Father with your whole heart. This makes Him happiest of all.

Dear Lord, I want to bring joy to Your heart. I really, really do.
I pray that my behavior always pleases You, Daddy God.

ETERNAL LIFE

Surely goodness and lovingkindness will follow me all the days of my life, and I will dwell in the house of the LORD forever.
PSALM 23:6 NASB

Have you ever thought about the word *eternity*? It will totally blow your mind if you stop to think about it. Eternity goes on forever and ever and ever. It has no beginning and it has no end. When we get to heaven, we will experience eternity. We won't be thinking about how many years we might live, because we will live. . .forever!

What an amazing thought! Forever! No ending time. It would be like going to a movie that never ever came to an end. . .it just kept going and going. That's how our lives are going to be in heaven.

So what do we have to do to experience this "forever" kind of life? How do we get to heaven? We have to ask Jesus to come and live in our hearts. Then we'll get to share eternity with Him in heaven. What an amazing adventure that will be.

Father, I can't wait to spend eternity with You.
We will be together forever. . .and forever. . .and forever! Wow!

GRATITUDE

This is the day that the LORD has made;
let us rejoice and be glad in it.
PSALM 118:24 ESV

Do you know what it means to be grateful? It means you're thankful. . .for everything! You're thankful for your family, your home, and your friends. You're thankful for the food you get to eat and the clothes you wear to school. Most of all, you're grateful to know that God loves you, no matter what.

A girl who's truly grateful never gets tired of saying "Thank you!" She appreciates her parents for all they do, and she's thankful to teachers and friends at church for giving of their time. She's not just saying "Thanks" to win extra credit with everyone; she's really, truly grateful!

Gratitude is something we can develop over time, so ask God to give you an attitude of gratitude. He will do it! Before you know it, your heart will be filled to overflowing with thankfulness for God's many blessings.

Father, my heart is so full right now! I'm so grateful for all
You've done for me. I feel so blessed to have a wonderful life,
a great family, and people who love me. Thank You!

172

GENTLENESS

Let your gentleness be evident to all. The Lord is near.

PHILIPPIANS 4:5 NIV

What do you think of when you hear the word *gentle*? Do you think of how you act around a newborn baby? Do you think that gentleness means weakness?

A gentle person isn't weak. She's actually very strong on the inside. She's so strong, in fact, that she knows how to control herself so that she doesn't hurt others. She doesn't raise her voice, yelling at her brothers and sisters. She doesn't overreact when her mom tells her to do something. She responds with a gentle, soothing voice.

How do we become gentle? We have to ask God for a new heart, one that is softened toward Him. A soft heart will help us be kinder and gentler to others. We can't do this on our own. Only God can soften our hearts. So ask Him! And He'll do it. Why? Because He wants to help you be the best you can be.

Lord, I want to be gentle inside and out.
Soften my heart so that I can respond to
others in a more loving way!

FIRM STEPS

The steps of a good man are led by the Lord. And He is happy in his way.
When he falls, he will not be thrown down, because the Lord holds his hand.

PSALM 37:23–24 NLV

If you were asked to run in a long race, what kind of shoes would you wear? Sandals? Dressy church shoes? Crocs? Tennis shoes? You would pick the kind of shoe that would keep you the safest, wouldn't you?

God wants our steps to be safe. He wants us to run our race with courage, not worrying that we might trip and fall every other minute. So how do we run with courage? How do we keep our steps firm? We have to run toward Him, with our eyes "fixed" on Him. (This means we never look to the right or the left but only to God.)

How do we look to God? We read our Bible and then obey what we've read. We pray and ask God to show us what to do during tough times. We remind ourselves every day that He is leading and guiding us and that we have nothing to fear.

No matter what kind of shoes you choose to wear today, God can make your steps firm. You can run safely. Just remember to run straight to Him!

Lord, I get it! You want me to run to You. . .for everything!
My life is a race, but You're standing there, guiding me
every step of the way. I'm keeping my eyes on You!

STRONG FAITH

Jesus turned, and seeing her he said, "Take heart, daughter; your faith
has made you well." And instantly the woman was made well.
MATTHEW 9:22 ESV

Most of us would say that we have strong faith. However, when the rough times come, our faith is tested, and sometimes we don't pass the test.

Here's an example: Imagine you're doing great in school; then. . .bam! Your favorite teacher moves away and a new teacher takes her place. The new teacher doesn't know that you're a good student. She doesn't even really know you at all. Maybe she doesn't treat you as kindly as the last teacher. She's not the let's-have-fun-while-we're-learning sort. Your grades start to slip. So does your attitude. Before long you don't even like going to school anymore. You don't have faith to believe that God can turn the situation around. You just want your old teacher back.

Get the point? If we truly have the faith that the Lord offers to us, we can believe that the situation with the new teacher can work out great. So don't give up. Keep on believing. Keep your faith strong, no matter what.

Father, I get it. My faith isn't always as strong as I say—or think—it is.
I give up pretty easily sometimes. Remind me that You can
work out everything. . .if I just keep believing!

CONSEQUENCES

For the wages of sin is death, but the free gift of God
is eternal life in Christ Jesus our Lord.
ROMANS 6:23 ESV

What comes to mind when you hear the word *consequences*? Do you think of when your mom gave you a time-out because of bad behavior? Are you reminded of a time when your kid sister was grounded for doing something really bad?

Having consequences means you have to pay a price for your actions. Here's an example: Imagine it's a really cold day outside. It's snowing like crazy. You decide to head outside and go sledding with your friends, but you don't want to take the time to put on a coat. You run and play, shivering the whole time. When you get back in the house, you're shaking like a leaf and you don't feel so good. The next day you wake up with a fever and a sore throat. These are the consequences of playing in the snow without a coat on!

Every action has a reaction. When you do one thing, something else happens. When you treat people nicely, they react by treating you nicely. (What lovely consequences!) When you treat others badly, they treat you badly. (What icky consequences.) There's always a price to pay, good or bad. But how lovely that Jesus paid the ultimate price for you.

Father, thank You for teaching me about consequences.
I know that I still have a lot to learn. Please help me on this journey.

My Fortress

But I will sing of your strength, in the morning I will sing of your love;
for you are my fortress, my refuge in times of trouble.

PSALM 59:16 NIV

. . . .

Many, many years ago, people lived in villages that were surrounded by massive stone walls that took years to build. Why did they work so hard to put up huge walls? To keep the enemy out. Those walls were a fortress—a way to keep the people safe and secure.

Did you know that you have a fortress? It's true! Your fortress isn't a stone wall or a huge gate. The Lord is your fortress! He's like a giant wall, keeping the enemy away from you. Cool, right? He won't let the enemy take you down. Oh, you might still go through tough times, but with God as your protector, you will come out of it okay in the end because He's your fortress and won't ever quit looking out for you, day or night.

Isn't it exciting to know that God has His safety net all around you? Praise Him for that! What a powerful God we serve!

. . . .

Father, thank You for being my fortress (my strong wall of protection).
I know You're there looking out for me so I don't have to be afraid. Whew!

THE DARKEST VALLEY

Even though I walk through the darkest valley, I will fear no evil,
for you are with me; your rod and your staff, they comfort me.
PSALM 23:4 NIV

If you've read Psalm 23 before, you've already seen words like those in today's scripture: "Even though I walk through the darkest valley, I will fear no evil."

Have you ever tried to walk in the darkness? Maybe you got out of bed in the middle of the night to go to the bathroom and stubbed your toe on the edge of the bed. Or maybe you tripped over the cat. Maybe you ran into the dresser and banged up your knee.

Walking in the dark isn't fun, but here's God's promise: when you go through "dark" seasons (and we all do), He won't leave you. You don't have to be afraid. True, you might not be able to see where you're going, but if you hold tight to God's hand, you can be sure He can see what's ahead. He's got great night vision! He knows how to keep you safe and secure and will guide you back to the light. Trust Him. Just trust Him.

Father, sometimes I go through rough times and I feel like I can't see what's coming next. It seems kind of dark! I'm so glad You are guiding me and that Your night vision is awesome!

LET'S GO TO CHURCH!

"For where two or three gather in my name, there am I with them."
MATTHEW 18:20 NIV

Going to church on Sundays isn't something we do so that we can get a sticker on a chart or some sort of brownie points with God. It's not even something we do because we *have* to. (Face it, some girls go to church because Mom or Dad says they have to.)

God wants you to want to go to church. He wants you to be as excited about going as you would be about a birthday party or Christmas morning. Going to church is the best way to take a break from your schoolwork, your troubles, your everyday life, and totally focus on Him. In church you can learn how to listen to His voice, how to pray, and how to worship. You also learn how to fellowship. To *fellowship* means to hang out with other Christians who love God as much as you do.

So are you excited about going to church? If not, ask God to make you excited! He has a lot of wonderful things in store for you. It's not just about lessons and sermons. It's about getting close to your heavenly Father and learning how to trust Him. What are you waiting for? Let's go to church!

Father, I love going to church, and not just because
I have fun hanging out with my friends. Mostly,
I'm excited about hanging out with You!

PRIORITIES

"But seek first the kingdom of God and his righteousness, and all these things will be added to you."
MATTHEW 6:33 ESV

Have you ever heard the word *priorities*? To have your priorities right means you know what's most important, and you do those things first.

Here's an example: Maybe you wake up on a Saturday morning and have a lot of things to do. You want to play with your friends, but your mom wants you to clean out your closet while she's shopping at the grocery store. You also need to change the cat's litter box. Oh, and you should probably send that thank-you note to your grandmother for the sweater she sent you for your birthday.

How do you know what's most important? Start with what you've been told to do. Always do that first. Then do what's next important, and so on. So here's how your day might go: Start by tidying up your closet like your mom said. And clean the cat's litter box. (Icky!) Then write that thank-you note. After that, you can go play with your friends, if your mom's okay with that.

Spiritually you have priorities too. Jesus tells you to first seek Him and do things His way. Then everything else will take care of itself.

When you've got your earthly and heavenly priorities right, every job gets done. Mom's happy. The cat's happy. Grandma's happy. You're happy. . . and God's happy!

Lord, thanks for the reminder that I need to have my priorities right! I want to do things in the right order so that everyone can say, "Job well done, girl!"

TELL THE TRUTH

*The LORD hates those who tell lies but is pleased
with those who keep their promises.*

PROVERBS 12:22 NCV

Have you ever told a lie? Maybe it wasn't a big one but a teensy-tiny not-quite-true one. Here's the thing. In God's eyes, even a little lie is big. He is very clear in His Word, the Bible, that we should be truth tellers, no matter how hard it might be.

Are you a truth teller? Here's a little test. Let's say you accidentally broke a lamp in the living room. Your mom sees the broken lamp and blames it on your new puppy. You don't say a word. You just let your mom think the puppy did it. No one will ever find out, right? After all, the puppy can't speak up and defend himself.

In a situation such as this, staying silent is the very same thing as lying. It's true. You have to speak up and tell the truth, even when you know you'll probably be disciplined. Still, wouldn't you rather face a little discipline for a broken lamp than feel guilty in your heart for lying to your mom? The truth will always set you free—so speak up, girl!

Father, I don't always tell the whole truth. Sometimes I leave things out or totally stay silent when I should speak up. Please help me to be a truth teller, even during the hard times!

THE COMFORTER

And I will pray the Father, and he shall give you another
Comforter, that he may abide with you for ever.
JOHN 14:16 KJV

Have you ever cuddled up under a blanket or comforter on a cold winter's night? There's something so wonderful about snuggling up, safe and sound. You can sleep better and feel cozy.

Did you know that God's Spirit lives inside of you when you ask Jesus to live in your heart? It's true! And His Spirit is called "the Comforter." He's like a warm, cozy blanket on a chilly night. Imagine God wrapping His arms around you and snuggling you close. That's what it's like when the Holy Spirit brings comfort. You feel safe and secure, wrapped in His loving arms.

If you're feeling lonely or afraid, just say these words: "Thank You, God, for Your Spirit. I'm so glad the Comforter lives inside of me!" There! Doesn't that feel good?

Dear Lord, I'm so grateful for Your Spirit. I feel so safe, so secure, so cozy.
Ah, what a wonderful, comforting God You are!

LOOK TO THE HEAVENS!

The heavens declare the glory of God;
the skies proclaim the work of his hands.

PSALM 19:1 NIV

Have you ever gone outside at night and stared up at the stars in the sky above? When the sky is really dark, the stars are brighter than ever. They twinkle, twinkle against the black sky—how they shimmer with light! Don't they look teensy-tiny up there, sparkling away?

The stars are actually huge! They're giant creations that only look teensy-tiny from Earth! The stars and the moon and the sun were placed in the sky by your heavenly Father. Why? Well, they serve a purpose, of course! They provide guidance for sailors, regulate the tides, warm up the planet, and stuff like that. But they're also there to show God's glory, His majesty. If you close your eyes really tight—c'mon and close 'em—you can almost imagine them singing the praises of God, telling the wonders of their awesome Creator.

The next time you look up into the sky and see a bright white star or a golden moon, pause a minute. Close your eyes. Think about God seated on His throne in heaven and seated on the throne of your heart. Doesn't just thinking about Him bring a huge smile to your face?

Well? What are you waiting for? Praise Him!

Lord, whenever I get so busy that I forget You are a wonder-working God, remind me to look up at the stars in the sky. They are a constant reminder that You are majestic. You can do anything, Father!

AS WE FORGIVE OTHERS

"For if you forgive other people when they sin against you, your heavenly Father will also forgive you. But if you do not forgive others their sins, your Father will not forgive your sins."

MATTHEW 6:14–15 NIV

There are so many reasons why we need to forgive others. Not doing so isn't just bad for those who have wronged us; it's bad for us! It messes up everything.

The main reason we need to be quick to forgive is this: God forgives us as we forgive others. He's watching to see if we're going to be gracious and forgive others first.

Ouch! Think about that. If someone hurts us and we refuse to forgive them, God might choose not to forgive us. Scary thought, isn't it? We don't ever want to be in that position. We definitely need forgiveness from God for the many times we mess up. So that means we have to forgive others, even when we don't feel like it. Certainly, it will be hard at times, but it will be worth it, for sure!

God, I don't always feel like forgiving others, but I definitely need to be forgiven for the times I've made mistakes. Help me, Lord, to forgive just like You forgive!

BORN AGAIN

Jesus answered and said to [Nicodemus], "Truly, truly, I say to you,
unless one is born again he cannot see the kingdom of God."
JOHN 3:3 NASB

Have you ever heard the term *born again*? Maybe you've heard it but don't know what it means. To be born again doesn't mean you have to go back inside your mommy's tummy and come out all over again. (Imagine that!) It means that God can give you a new life, different from the one you were living before.

To live this new life, you have to believe that God sent His Son to this earth. You have to believe that Jesus—God's Son—lived a sinless (blameless) life and then carried all of our sins (mistakes) to the cross. When Jesus died on the cross, He took our shame so that we could live forever with Him someday in heaven. That's the best gift of all! We will talk more about how to accept this gift in the next devotion, but spend a little time looking up the words *born again*. Talk to your parents or Sunday school teacher about them and then get ready! God wants all of His girls to be born, not just once, but twice! What are you waiting for, sweet girl? Now is the time!

Father, I'm curious about what it means to be born again.
I can't wait to learn more!

WRAPPING It UP

*To sum up, all of you be harmonious, sympathetic,
brotherly, kindhearted, and humble in spirit.*

1 PETER 3:8 NASB

. . . .

If you could take all of the things we've learned in this devotional book and put them in one little sentence, what would it say? God wants us to love Him and love others. He doesn't just want us to love in a so-so sort of way, but in an all-out sort of way. The all-out kind of love isn't prideful. It's not mean-spirited. It gets along with others, even when they are rude to us.

Most important, we need to have an all-out love for God. This means that we go on loving Him even when life doesn't make sense. We trust. We obey. We follow Him every day of our lives, not giving in when others try to pull us away from what we believe.

God loves you, precious girl. He really, really does. And His love for you will never end. Love Him back. If you haven't already done this, ask His Son, Jesus, to come and live in your heart, to be the Lord of your life. It will be the best decision you ever make.

. . . .

Lord Jesus, I ask You to come and live in my heart today. Change my life!
I give myself to You. Be my Lord and Savior. Help me to love
others and to love You every single day of my life. Amen.

SCRIPTURE INDEX

Old Testament

Genesis
1:1–2.................................13
1:20.............................. 122
1:27...............................19
2:2–3............................. 111
2:21–22 155
9:13 143
24:45 136
29 146
29:25 146

Exodus
14:21–22........................8
20:1–3 51
32:1 140

Numbers
14:11..............................12

Judges
16:6.............................100

Ruth
1:16..............................118

1 Samuel
1:10............................. 163

16:7 110
17:4.............................. 62
17:26 24

1 Chronicles
16:9...............................41

2 Chronicles
20 41

Esther
4:14 28

Job
8:21 101

Psalms
9:2 40
16:8 133
16:9 .... 67, 70
18:2 20
18:3 48
19:1 183
23.................................178
23:4.....................139, 178
23:6............................. 171
27:1............................. 56
30:5.............................142
30:11...........................144

31:24......................47
37:5......................73
37:23–24..................174
47:1......................21
59:16.....................177
62:1–2....................112
62:11.....................139
86:15.....................169
90:17......................17
101:2–3...................108
103:1.....................132
103:3.....................139
116:1.....................139
118:24....................172
119:78....................159
119:105.....................5
139:13–14..................22
145:4.....................147
147:5......................37

PROVERBS

1:7.......................139
1:8–9......................99
3:6.......................134
3:12......................102
3:24......................113
4:10–11...................149
4:20......................107
11:2.......................30
12:19......................79
12:22.....................181

14:23......................94
15:20......................96
18:24.....................151
22:6......................137
25:21......................60
31:30......................83

ECCLESIASTES

3:1.......................114

ISAIAH

26:3–4....................130
26:4......................139
54:17......................15
61:4......................117
64:8........................9

JEREMIAH

1:5........................25
1:7........................11
29:11......................39
29:13–14...................18

JONAH

1:3........................61

New Testament

MATTHEW

5:13.......................71

5:14 14
5:16 129
6:14–15 184
6:33 180
6:34 82
7:9, 11 120
7:24–25 153
9:22 175
10:31 141
12:33 68
13:44 75
14:25–26 16
18:12 93
18:15 119
18:20 179
22:37–39 158

MARK

12:30–31 27
12:31 29
16:15 55

LUKE

1:37 157
1:41–42 125
1:46–47 165
2:11 80
5:16 106
10:33 154
12:2 97
13:24 148

14:28 150
15:10 84
15:20 156
16:19–21 85
21:3–4 167
22:26 168

JOHN

3:3 185
3:16 123
14:2 138
14:15 42
14:16 182
15:18 63
16:33 66
18:25 32
21:7 26

ACTS

20:35 58

ROMANS

3:23–24 7
6:23 176
7:19–20 54
8:16–17 90
8:38–39 38
12:2 131
12:3 127
15:4 98
15:5–6 161

15:13 44

1 Corinthians
13:7 164
16:13 10

2 Corinthians
1:20 139
5:7 46
6:18 116

Ephesians
1:4 59
4:2–3 124
4:29 135
4:31–32 128

Philippians
2:3 81
2:4 162
2:14–16 45
3:13–14 87
3:14 36
4:4 139
4:5 173
4:13 109
4:19 166

Colossians
3:8 50
3:14 31

3:23 86

1 Thessalonians
3:7 74
5:12 91
5:16–18 145

1 Timothy
6:6–8 57
6:10 95
6:12 152

2 Timothy
1:6 53
2:15 34
3:14 33

Philemon
1:4 115

Hebrews
11:30 105
12:1–2 23
13:5 .... 104, 139

JAMES
1:2–3 89
1:19–20 77
2:1 65
2:2–4 43
4:11 88

5:18......................160

1 Peter
1:8–9.....................126
1:17 103
3:8 186
5:7.........................121

2 Peter
1:17 170

1 John
1:5–6...................64
1:9.........................92
2:9–10...................35
2:15 72
3:1.........................49
3:16 76

3 John
1:11 52

Revelation
5:11–12 69
10:9.........................78

ABOUT THE AUTHOR

Janice Hanna Thompson is the author of over one-hundred books for the Christian market. She lives in the Houston area near her family.

BiGHEARTED PEOPLE

Let each of you look not only to his own interests,
but also to the interests of others.

PHILIPPIANS 2:4 ESV

Don't you love generous, bighearted people? They're always looking out for others, ready to meet needs and extend a hand to help. Maybe your parents are generous, always wanting to pay the bill for others. Maybe your grandpa likes to give generously to his grandkids.

It's so much fun to watch generous people care for others. They don't make a big show of their giving. They're simply there at the right moment, ready to help.

What about you? Are you generous? Oh, I know, you might not have a lot of money to give away, but are you generous in other ways? Do you share your toys? Do you argue when you don't get to watch the show on TV that you want? Do you make a big deal when you don't get your way? Generous girls are always looking out for the other person. They're definitely not selfish. They want to bring a smile to the face of a friend or family member.

Ah, generosity! What a lovely gift! You can give it to those you love today! Nothing will make God's heart happier.

Father, show me how I can be more generous. I want to be known
as someone who cares more about the needs of others
than my own. Help me be that, Lord.

LOOKiNG AT THE GLASS

May the God who gives endurance and encouragement give you the same
attitude of mind toward each other that Christ Jesus had, so that
with one mind and one voice you may glorify the God
and Father of our Lord Jesus Christ.

ROMANS 15:5–6 NIV

Some folks say the glass is half empty. Others say it's half full. Still others say the glass is twice as big as it should be! What do you say?

Imagine you're looking at a glass with water in it. The water is about to the halfway point. Would you say the glass is half empty or half full? Different people would give different answers, wouldn't they?

It's always best to look at life with a half-full attitude. The half-full girl is positive. She's always seeing the good in things. The half-empty girl is a whiner. A complainer. She sees all the negative things.

Are you positive or negative? Be honest! When life gets hard, are you whining and complaining or seeing the glass as half full? Time to check your attitude, girl!

Dear Lord, I want to be positive! I want to be one of those girls who brightens everyone's day. Help me to see the glass as always half full, never half empty!